Reflections of Our Gentle Warriors

ISBN: 978-1-63490-825-2

Published by BookLocker.com, Inc., Bradenton, Florida, U.S.A.

Printed on acid-free paper.

BookLocker.com, Inc.
2015

First Edition

Reflections of Our Gentle Warriors

Brad Hoopes

To

Alex and Molly
I love you dearly

And to my parents.
Thank you for your love and support, as well as for always believing in me, even when I didn't.

Acknowledgements

Reflections of Our Gentle Warriors is an extension of a very passionate project of mine to interview and preserve the stories of veterans. I am indebted to all the men and women who have sat down with me and shared their stories. In particular, the ones who allowed me to share their stories in this book. There are so many more I could share, which is only the very tip of the iceberg of the stories out there. Thanks to Northern Colorado Honor Flight for allowing me to be part of this very special program. Many of my connections for the interviews came through Honor Flight. I want to thank the following writers from whose advice I have sought out over the years: Jerry Whiting, who does incredible work; Sheryl Jones; Larry Krantz; Irene Hannigan; Diggs Brown; Bob McDonnell; Bill Lampere; Jean Messinger; Teresa Funke; and Jonna Doolittle Hoppes. Thank you Andrew Manriquez, Jerry Whiting, Dick Olson, and Ken Bledsoe for the endless hours of pure enjoyment sitting in the shade under the wing of a B-17 at the WWII appreciation weekends, sharing our mutual love of this history and admiration for the people who served in it. Thank you Dave Tuttle, Becky Haley, Stephanie McHale-Donvan, and Jean Messinger for reading rough transcripts and offering your corrections and feedback. To my special friend and mentor, Dr. Robin Herron, for your friendship, advice, insights, and support. Thank you to all my friends and family who kept pushing and cheering me on to write this book. Lastly, I would like to thank my editor, Hilary Handelsman for all your hard work and advice.

Table of Contents

Introduction

I first started interviewing veterans and preserving their stories a number of years ago. The project represented a convergence of several interests: I love history, I love listening to people tell their stories, and I have deep respect and awe for what veterans have done and continue to do. I had just finished reading Tom Brokaw's book, *The Greatest Generation*, and had also learned about the Library of Congress's Veterans History Project. I thought to myself, "Why not try to do something on a local level?" I went out, bought a video camera, and began interviewing. It has proven to be a fascinating and fulfilling experience.

The main objective of my project is to make sure that the veterans' families have a permanent record of their stories, never to be lost or forgotten. A secondary objective is to make sure a copy of these stories is preserved by public institutions so present and future generations can learn about these people. Depending on when you are reading this book, there may not be any World War II veterans still living. As I write, more than five hundred veterans are passing away each day and taking their stories with them.

These veterans were from a humble generation. They went off to war, came home, and moved on with their lives without missing a beat. Most had never told their story—or only bits of it, if they had talked about it at all—before sitting down with me, and they were all in their eighties or older when I interviewed them. A prime example was a man who was badly injured in the fighting on Iwo Jima and was the sole survivor of his unit. Years later his son approached him and asked his father to take him to a costume shop. When the man asked his son why, his son said he needed an army outfit for a play he was in at school. The father asked, "Why don't you use mine?" The son didn't even know he had been in the army, let alone his incredible story!

The downside to coming back and moving right along with life was that many of these men suffered from what we now know as PTSD; they held in emotions and experiences that in many cases they carried with them for sixty-five years or more. Very seldom did I leave an interview where the veteran or I—or both of us—had not cried. When I started this project, I thought that it would primarily benefit the veterans' families, which of course it has proven to do. But I found out that it often benefited the veteran himself. I once got a call from the wife of a veteran the morning after I had interviewed him. She thanked me and told me that the previous night had been the first time in sixty years that her husband had slept through the night. Once, after asking a standard question about whether the veteran had ever been able to travel back to where he had served, I received an answer that is still seared in my brain: "Why should I? I'm there almost every night." I still think with sadness of the veteran so wracked with arthritis that it takes him five minutes to cross a room, yet his wife says he flies out of bed like Superman every night because of nightmares. So many times I heard, "I can't remember what I had for breakfast this morning, but I remember where I was on August 8, 1943." So often I wish it was the other way around for these people, and they could say, "I had bacon and eggs for breakfast this morning, but I just don't remember being in that foxhole with my feet frozen solid . . . or the time my ship was attacked . . . or that horrible mission over Berlin . . . or the day my best buddy was killed." On the flip side, another woman told me that her husband walked around for days after the interview, his chest puffed out with pride. Most of these men will tell you that they didn't do anything. I hope this veteran listened to his own words and realized that, yes, indeed, he did do something.

Do I think that some of these stories may have been embellished? Yes, I am sure they have been. I am sure that some of the facts are incorrect as well. I choose to overlook any embellishments simply because, given what these men have done, I believe they are entitled to exaggerate a little bit. If some of the facts are incorrect, I think this is largely due to the fog of war and the fact that the veterans were recounting stories sixty-five years after they happened. I was never after the facts, anyway, since these are all collected in the history books. I wanted to capture the human perspective and experience, which I believe will powerfully enhance the facts and figures.

There were two aspects of these veterans' experiences that I want to emphasize as a background to these stories. The first is the world they came from. Most of these people had never traveled more than fifty miles from home while growing up. They really only knew their immediate family, friends, and surroundings. There was no Internet cable TV with 300+ channels and 24/7 news coverage. Their sources for information about the outside world were maybe a *National Geographic* magazine in the library and the radio that they listened to at night. They were going off to an unknown experience in what was to them a largely unknown world.

The second aspect of their experiences, and one I still haven't been able to get my head around, is that they were just kids—eighteen, nineteen, twenty years old. I look at what my biggest worries or responsibilities were at that age: that math test on Wednesday . . . would that cute girl in English class ever go out with me . . . oh, and most important, what's going on Friday night? What was your personal world like at that age? These "kids" were thrown into situations—often sheer hell—where they were forced to assume enormous responsibility.

Due to the limitations of my location and demographics, there are a number of stories I was unable to collect that would have rounded out an overview of this important period in history. The stories of African-Americans, for example. They made contributions to the war for this country while still being treated as second-class citizens both in the armed forces and often back home. Another bleak page in our history was our treatment of Japanese-Americans. Some of the most decorated units overseas were Japanese-American, and they served while their families and friends were behind barbed wire in America. Finally, I wish I could have covered more thoroughly the incredible role women played in winning the war, both in the service and on the home front. I hope this book will prompt readers to go out and learn more about this truly pivotal era in American history.

I also hope that if you never got the chance to hear the story of someone who was special to you, maybe you'll come across a story in this book of someone who served in the same unit or on the same ship or who had the same type of duty and that it will give you some sense of what they experienced. My most fervent wish, however, is that you will seek out your father, grandfather, favorite uncle, or next-door neighbor to have them you tell their story or that you will tell your story, if you have one!

I hope this book will give you insight into where this generation came from, who they were, and what they experienced.

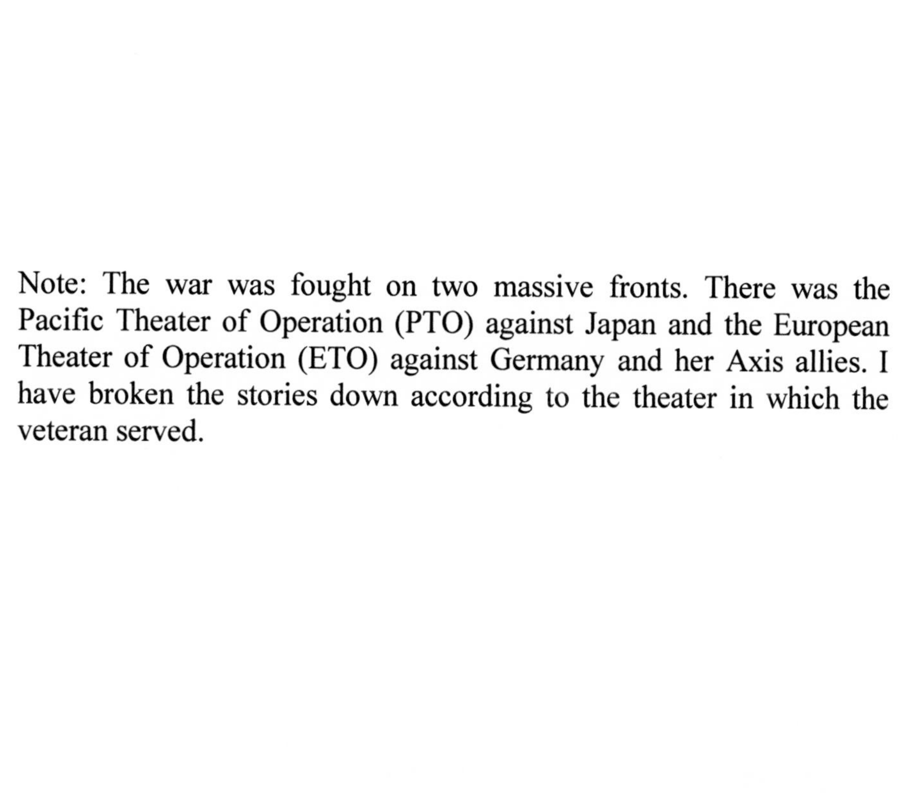

Note: The war was fought on two massive fronts. There was the Pacific Theater of Operation (PTO) against Japan and the European Theater of Operation (ETO) against Germany and her Axis allies. I have broken the stories down according to the theater in which the veteran served.

Pacific Theater
(PTO)

Brought It Back

The family farm in Kansas was the center of David Allen's universe for the first twenty-one years of his life. At this time, during the first half of the twentieth century, people seldom traveled more than fifty miles from their homes. A trip into Wichita was a big event. But over the next three years, David would find himself in the Mojave Desert, the paradise setting of Hawaii, the jungles of New Guinea and the Philippines, and finally on the peninsula of Korea. His war experiences would fundamentally change his life.

Because of his responsibilities on the farm, David could easily have gotten an agriculture deferment when he received his draft notice, but he declined to do so and went off to basic training. After training, he was assigned to the Army's 6th Engineers Battalion. The battalion boarded trains and headed to the Mojave Desert for maneuvers. Based on their training location, everyone was certain they were heading for Africa. This assumption was proven wrong when they moved up to San Francisco and boarded ships heading west past the Golden Gate Bridge.

Their first stop was Hawaii. Here they took training in jungle warfare and worked on a number of construction projects. Once again they again loaded onto ships and continued west, landing in New Guinea. The heat and humidity was crushing. "When we arrived, it was 120 degrees and raining," David recalls. He spent the next eleven months there as the 6th did its part to drive the Japanese out of New Guinea.

The responsibility of the combat engineers was to build the infrastructure to get the troops and equipment to the battle. They moved right behind the spearhead troops on the front line, often building roads and bridges in the midst of the fighting. A couple of times they actually found themselves ahead of US forces and behind enemy lines.

The 6th followed the war as it moved north to Japan. Next they took part in the invasion of Luzon in the Philippines. General MacArthur fulfilled the promise he made—"I shall return"—when he evacuated the Philippines two years earlier after the Japanese invasion. David actually met the general up close. While working on a road, a jeep stopped right in front of him. In the jeep was MacArthur, corncob pipe and all. Another memory was going to help the prisoners, many from the Bataan Death March, at the recently liberated prisoner of war camp. "We loaded up all the food, cigarettes, and candy we could for them. But no sooner did we hand it out than the POWs gave it all away to the locals in gratitude for their help during those terrible years. These guys were nothing but skin and bones."

David was training for the planned invasion of the Japanese homeland when news of the Japanese surrender broke. It was a huge relief, as he had seen firsthand that the Japanese fought to the bitter end and seldom surrendered. He was certain he would not have survived the invasion if it had gone ahead. With the war over, he was transferred to Korea as part of the occupation forces there. He was only there a month when he accumulated enough points to come home.

David brought a lot back home with him from his war experiences, both good and bad. He experienced a malaria attack on his wedding day and spent the next couple of weeks in the hospital. He adopted the "can-do" attitude of the combat engineers and not only used it successfully throughout his own life but also imparted it to his children, who are all very successful. The most important thing he brought back, though, was his strong religious faith. David said that while sitting in a foxhole in New Guinea during a terrifying artillery barrage, he turned his life over to Jesus Christ, and this strong faith has been the focal point of his life to this day.

David Allen

War and Park Service

Ken Ashley was in college studying forestry when Pearl Harbor was bombed. After the holidays, he and a buddy went to enlist in the Marines and were put into the Navy's V-7 program, which allowed them to finish college. When asked why he chose the Marines, he says he can't really remember, but he thinks it had to do with the image of the Marines in Hollywood movies.

Ken graduated from college in 1943 and immediately shipped off for basic training and Officer's Candidate School (OCS). He had a short leave before additional training, so he went back to see his college sweetheart, Ethel, and they got engaged. He had a short leave after training and before he left to go overseas. He and Ethel contemplated getting married but thought it was best to wait until he returned home—if he returned.

Ken shipped off to the Pacific as a replacement officer and landed in New Caledonia. From there he went to Guadalcanal and then farther north to the island of Vella Lavella. He was only on that island one night, but that night was very significant in his war experience. While there he ran into a classmate from OCS, who told him about an opening in his unit, the 8th 155 Gun Battalion. Ken was accepted into that unit, and by joining it he accumulated five extra points, which, after the war ended, meant the difference between being transferred to China or being able to come home.

Ken says, "I was lucky not to be one of those Marines that landed in Higgins boats and stormed the beaches." His positions in the two battles he was involved in weren't any easier, though.

His first battle was the invasion of Peleliu, an island that is part of the island nation of Palau. The strategy was that the guns used for long-range shelling would go onto Peleliu. Ken would accompany the Army to the island of Angaur, about nine miles offshore, as a forward observer, and radio coordinates back to the guns in support of the battle on that island. The fighting on Peleliu proved so vicious, however, that the guns never got on shore. Ken rejoined his unit, and when they were eventually able to get ashore, he suggested that they lower the guns, which normally lobbed shells up in the air, and fire directly into caves in the cliffs, which were filled with Japanese. Ken would be awarded a medal for this idea. Being only 300 yards away and below the caves, however, they were under constant sniper fire.

Ken's other battle was the battle of Okinawa, where he was an aerial observer. For a three-week period he flew twice a day in a slow-moving Stinson L-5 a couple of hundred feet over enemy territory. With the Japanese firing at him, not to mention the Navy, with its big guns and thirty-six battalions firing into this area, it was an extremely dangerous mission. He was awarded the Air Medal for his efforts.

Not all Ken's experiences were bad. He can laugh now about the time, after the war ended, when a typhoon was bearing down on Okinawa. Everyone was told to evacuate the camp and head to the hills. But Chicago was playing in the seventh game of the World Series, and Ken and a buddy, rabid Cubs fans, weren't about to miss it, so they stayed behind to listen to the game on the radio. The typhoon hit, completely destroying the camp. They made it out unscathed, but they never did hear the game, and, to make matters worse, the Cubs lost.

Ken returned home, and, after two and half years apart, he and Ethel got married. He went on to have a successful career with the National Park Service. One memorable assignment for him was going back to Peleliu more than forty years later to evaluate it as a potential national park.

Ken Ashley

Those Hands

To me, Ken Buffington is the perfect poster boy for his generation. He grew up amidst the struggles of the Great Depression and living on the edge of the Dust Bowl, heeded the call to go off and save the world during WWII, and then, without skipping a beat, returned home and worked hard to build something for his family, his community, and his country. These back-to-back struggles and hardships tempered him and his generation into what Tom Brokaw has called the Greatest Generation.

Growing up on a farm on the plains of western Nebraska was hard enough, but these ordinary hardships were compounded by the double whammy of the Great Depression and the Dust Bowl, which raged through the area for ten years. Ken moved into town during the school year to attend high school, living in a converted chicken coop and eating cold pancakes every day. At the end of his senior year, Ken was looking forward to the wheat crop coming in so that there would be money to go to college, only to watch a hail storm come along and—within minutes—destroy the wheat and his chances of going to college.

With the war under way and an older brother already in the Navy, Ken decided to enlist in the Navy as well. He said he enlisted in the service so he could do his part to get the job done as soon as possible and get back home. After training, he shipped out to Hawaii, where he went aboard the destroyer USS *Farenholt* as a radar man. His experience at sea started at the Solomon Islands and went up to Japan and the war's end. Along the way the *Farenholt* accrued thirteen battle stars. The ship was nearly sunk at the battle of Cape Esparance and was damaged in a number of other battles. Ken said he would never forget—and was still bothered by—the sight and smells as they removed the remains of sailors killed inside one of the big guns when it was hit. Ken himself was in the dangerous position of loading shells into one of the other large guns.

When the *Farenholt* returned to the West Coast for much-needed repairs, Ken took advantage of a ten-day furlough and rushed home to get married. With travel time eating up most of the ten days, it was a wedding he and his fiancée put together quickly, followed by a one-night honeymoon, before Ken headed back to the ship. It was a marriage that would last until his lovely Nina's death in 2003.

When the war ended, Ken returned home to Nina and immediately began trying to resume a life interrupted by war. He eventually got into the plumbing and heating business, in which he would go on to have a thirty-year career. After a long, physical day working in construction, he continued to be active once he got home from work. Family meant everything to him, and he was deeply involved in his kids' sports and school activities. Giving back to the community was also very important to him. He served on the city council, the volunteer fire department, and the American Legion Board. When he moved his family to Colorado to secure better educational opportunities for his kids, he helped start the local youth baseball league.

At Ken's funeral, his son gave a very moving eulogy—telling his father's life story through his memories of Ken's hands. They were strong hands, calloused from working on the farm in his youth, loading shells in the five-inch guns of the *Farenholt*, and working hard to support his family. They were hands that still found time to throw a baseball or help fix a bicycle seat. They were the hands of a man who, through hard work and perseverance, made it through some of the greatest struggles of the twentieth century and came out the other end to provide his family with a better life than he had growing up and to help make America into the greatest economy this world has ever seen.

Ken Buffington

Hate and Love

"It was all about hate, love, and living one day at a time." That is Hank Cornellisson's explanation of how he made it through his struggles during and after the war.

Like most of his generation, he first struggled through the difficulties caused by the Great Depression before the war. A year after he graduated from high school in Barnard, Kansas, a buddy suggested they join the Navy. The Navy wouldn't take them, so they went and talked to the Army recruiter. He said he would call if anything opened up, and a couple of weeks later he contacted them, saying there were two openings in the Army Air Corps in the Philippines. Hank and his buddy had just seen the movie *Mutiny on the Bounty* the night before and were up for the adventure. They signed up on September 6, 1939.

In October Hank, his buddy, and two others they met up with in Wichita departed from the United States for the Philippines. Hank would be the only one who came back. They sailed the Pacific and settled at Clark Air Base with the 28th Bomb Squadron in the exotic tropics of the Philippines. Hank became an airplane mechanic, and his buddy went into communications. Life was good. Local Filipinos worked in the barracks as houseboys, and Hank was able to send money home for college after his discharge. This idyllic life was shattered, however, on December 8, 1941.

Hank says they all knew for a year that war with Japan was inevitable, yet when the airfield was attacked that day, they were unprepared. Hank was walking from the barracks out to the flight line to work on a plane when Japanese bombers appeared and start bombing the base. Hank was trapped out in the open, hugging the ground, while gravel was being kicked up into his face by bullets from the fighter planes that followed the bombers, strafing the area. The attack finally ended, and the reality that this was war set in for Hank when he saw half of a soldier's body lying in the field.

Hank's unit stayed at the base for another three weeks and then retreated to Bataan. From there they withdrew to the southernmost island in the Philippines, Mindanao. At this point they were more or less out of supplies and were living off the land. When Gen. Wainwright surrendered the island, it was every man for himself, and many fled into the mountains. Hank somehow found himself driving a bus, looking for other soldiers to hook up with. Slowing down in a town, he soon found two Japanese soldiers on the running boards sticking bayonets into his ribs. He was now a prisoner and would go on to spend the rest of the war in Japanese prison camps.

Hank spent five months at a POW camp in the Philippines. Aside from not being given much food, they were treated fairly well by the Japanese, in contrast to what would follow. Hank remembers how beautiful and serene the bay was the day they left Mindanao. It is a vivid memory that has remained with him. After a stop in Manila, they began the trek across the China Sea to Japan. Sixteen hundred men were put into the hold of the Hell Ship *Torrori Maru*. "It was so crowded that if you wanted to lie down, your buddy had to stand up," Hank says. During the thirty-day journey, at least a person a day perished.

After landing in Japan, they took a train to a camp on the bay outside Tokyo, where they were forced to work on the docks. The Japanese moved prisoners around quite often to break them up. Hank was transferred to work at the brick factory, which was lucky for him because it was heated. From there he was moved to a camp near the Kawasaki steel mills. Every chance the prisoners got, they sabotaged the operations—by working very slowly and acting like they didn't know how to do something or by putting sand in the oil that ran the machines.

Conditions in the camps were beyond intolerable. They slept three men to a small bunk bed, rotating every night so that a different person slept in the middle for warmth. They were subject to severe beatings and punishments. Hank remembers a prisoner who was forced to stand in the cesspool up to his neck in waste all night. Their food consisted primarily of spoiled rice with worms and bugs in it and an occasional scrap of carrot or other vegetable. In a room of thirty men, Hank was the heaviest, at 116 pounds.

When asked how he made it through all of this, he says this is where the hate came in. "You went to bed at night praying that you would die. When you woke up in the morning, you said to yourself—I am going to hate these SOBs another day. Those who no longer had emotions of any sort still left in them usually went into a corner and died."

The steel mills and the camp were destroyed by American bombings, so the prisoners were moved to a camp in the mountains. It was there that they learned that huge bombs had been dropped on Japan and that the war had ended. The Air Force soon dropped supplies into the camp, but it would not be until September 6, six years to the day after he enlisted, that Hank was released from the camp.

He returned to San Francisco in October 1945, six years after he had left for what was supposed to be a two-year assignment. He spent 1,218 days as a prisoner. He went home to his family for a reunion he will never forget. His family had endured the first thirteen months of his captivity knowing only that the Army had listed his status as "unknown." After it was confirmed that he was a POW, they were finally able to exchange a couple of letters. He was sent home by the Army for a ninety-day furlough to recover. His mother's excellent cooking helped him regain the weight he had lost. He laughs as remembers how his mom once gave him a pail of food scraps and vegetable tops to throw outside in the trash. He looked at her and said, "But Mom, this would make a good soup." Working for his dad at the family nursery also helped him to gain back his strength. He was still full of various types of worms and once passed a tapeworm a foot and a half long and as thick as a pencil. Medicine from the Army helped clear that up.

Hank was now healed physically, but not mentally. He began drinking and had a problem with his temper. The military didn't truly understand such things as PTSD at that time and was not set up to provide the treatment men needed when they came home from war. People like Hank were on their own to deal with it. Hank figures that overcoming the trauma of being a prisoner was almost a twenty-year process. He began studying human behavior, and eventually he and his wife (whom he gives great credit for dealing with it all) began attending couples' weekend retreats sponsored by their church. Eventually they found themselves leading those retreats, and Hank realized that as he and his wife were helping others, he was also helping himself.

"This is where the love comes in," he says. "I completely removed hate from my life and replaced it fully with thoughts of love!"

Henry Cornellisson's POW picture

Floating City

Henry Detterer grew up in the small, quiet, landlocked farming community of Windsor, Colorado. Now in the Navy, he found himself halfway around the world at sea on a ship with three times the population as his hometown.

He quit school to enlist, as he felt it was his time to go. Sixty-three members of the congregation of the small church in his small town would serve in the war. Henry completed boot camp in Idaho and reported to Washington State for his assignment to the aircraft carrier USS *Yorktown*. Henry was coming aboard the second *Yorktown*, as the first one had been sunk during the battle of Midway. He remembers arriving to find the *Yorktown* in dry dock for repairs. Looking up at the massive ship, he said to himself, "There's no way that can float." It did indeed float, however, and after going down the coast to San Francisco for supplies, it headed west to the war zone in the Pacific.

Henry was assigned to the flight deck, prepping planes for takeoff and handling them when they returned. It was dangerous work, operating in fast-paced and hectic conditions among the sharp edges and whirling propellers of the planes, which were parked close together. Henry remembers the time a crew chief got chewed up by a propeller. There was no time to be scared or to grieve at that moment. They simply had to clean up the mess and keep on with the task of getting planes in the air.

The *Yorktown* was awarded eleven battle stars, and Henry was involved in six of those awards. Aircraft carriers were a prime target of the Japanese. Although they were surrounded by battleships, destroyers, and cruisers for protection, enemy planes did get through at times. In one attack, a plane managed to drop a bomb on the *Yorktown*, killing five and injuring twenty-six. One of those killed was another man from Windsor. Henry knew him back home, but they had never become friends until they found themselves on the ship together. Henry says they had had a conversation just days before his friend died in which the man said he didn't think he would make it through the war, and Henry had tried to convince him otherwise.

In addition to the dangers of being in a war zone, the *Yorktown* was caught in two major typhoons. Henry remembers being on the flight deck, which one minute was eighty feet above the water line, and the next minute was at the water line because the waves were so high. Three destroyers escorting the *Yorktown* were sunk during one of these storms.

Life on the *Yorktown*, when not in the midst of battle, was pretty good, according to Henry. It was virtually a floating city, with a mess hall, a library, a barbershop, and other amenities found in a city. Sleeping accommodations were comfortable. He found the food good most of the time, although having grown up on a farm, where everything is fresh, he never became accustomed to the powdered eggs and milk. His sister wrote him three times a week, for which Henry is grateful to this day, as getting those letters meant a lot to him.

When the Japanese surrendered, the *Yorktown* headed to Japan as part of the occupation forces. After landing in Tokyo Bay, the sailors were allowed liberty. Henry took advantage of this liberty, but because he did not feel comfortable venturing too far, he stayed fairly close to the ship. Subsequently he was transferred off the ship and given a new assignment on Guam, helping to destroy supplies and equipment. Instead of returning surplus supplies and equipment to the States, the government elected to destroy it. There were stories of tanks, planes, and other equipment and supplies simply being tossed overboard. A sad example of this was the hundreds of beautiful, high-quality flight jackets, which—despite the fact that he and practically everyone there wanted one—were put into a pile and burned.

Henry finally had enough points to return home. After the adventure of living on the sea and being half way around the world in tropical locations, Henry's feet were now firmly planted again in the soil of the Colorado prairie. He met Betty, who would become his wife, and together they raised a family and spent a lifetime successfully farming that soil.

Henry Detterer

Now, Git!

Don Draxler was nearing the end of the first semester of his freshman year at the University of Wisconsin when he arrived at his job at a chocolate shop on Sunday morning, December 7. When he stepped inside, all the guys were standing around. One asked Don which branch he was going to join. Don asked him what he was talking about and was told that the Japanese had bombed Pearl Harbor and that war with Japan had started. The attack was only hours old, and already everyone there had decided they were going to enlist.

A few weeks later Don left to go home to the family dairy farm for Christmas vacation. One of his intentions was to tell his parents of his plans to enlist. To his surprise, his father said he too wanted to enlist! A forty-three-year-old father of eight, he had had to stay home on the same family farm during World War I and didn't want to miss out serving in this war. Don's older brother would take over the farm, and after Don returned briefly to Madison to drop out of school and vacate his apartment, Don and his dad took off together for Camp Roberts, California.

They trained together in the same platoon, but in different squads. They both excelled and were the leaders of their respective squads. You would think a forty-three-year-old would have had a hard time keeping up with eighteen- and twenty-year-olds, but not this hardy dairy farmer! According to Don, he often out-did the others, and Don even remembers the times his father would carry Don's pack for him during runs and marches. They come to an impasse, however, when their training ended. Both Don and his dad fulfilled the requirements to go on to OCS, which Don wanted to do. But Don's dad just wanted to be a sergeant and didn't want to go. What complicated matters even more was that Don's mom, who never had much say in her husband's and sons decisions to serve, made them promise her they would stay together. The decision about whether or not to do this was soon made for them by a sad incident. The five Sullivan brothers were all killed while serving together on the same ship. Soon thereafter a rule was passed prohibiting family members from serving together. Don headed off to Georgia to OCS, and his dad went to the Aleutian Islands. While he never saw action there, he served twenty-seven months in harsh conditions and reached the rank of staff sergeant.

Don completed OCS and was commissioned as a lieutenant. Everyone in his class was given the option of going to Italy or the South Pacific. During school, Don and a man he met named Dave Gauge become close friends. So close, in fact, that they agreed to name their first sons after each other someday. In the meantime, Dave's brother had been in the Bataan Death March and was now a POW. Dave said he was heading to the PTO, hoping to bring his brother home, and of course Don decided to join him. They headed to Hawaii as replacement officers, and Dave was placed with a unit almost immediately, shipping out soon afterward. This was the last time Don and Dave saw each other, for Dave was killed in action. Don would eventually have five children, and his oldest son is named Dave.

Don was soon placed with the 27th Infantry Division, which up to this point had been guarding the Hawaiian Islands against a possible Japanese invasion. One day he was out at the shooting range with his men, who were "acting up." A colonel pulled up in his jeep, and Don went over to report in to him. The colonel, who was an imposing, six-foot-six-inch Kentuckian, asked Don how things were going. Don said that he was having a hard time keeping the men in order. The colonel, who had a riding crop in his hand, looked straight ahead and snapped it against his boots. What he said next was something Don would never forget—something that changed his life. "There ain't nothing you can't do if you fix your mind to! Now, git!" he drawled. Don soon had the men whipped into shape.

The 27th boarded ships and headed west to enter the fighting. Don's unit, Co. C of the 106th Infantry Regiment, was in reserve for the first two island invasions they were involved in. They spearheaded the next invasion in the Battle of Eniwetok Atoll. They were involved in fighting for three solid days to gain a half mile and defeat the Japanese. During this time a mortar shell hit the rim of a shell hole

Don was in, killing Don's assistant and another soldier. Don developed severe hearing loss as a result and received his first Purple Heart there. The next three weeks on the island were almost as bad as those three days of combat, as it was more than 100 degrees, and the island was covered with dead soldiers. The unit was put in charge of removing the dead and cleaning up the island. At night, coconut rats the size of cats came into the men's tents, seeking warmth.

The next invasion for Don and his company was the invasion of Saipan. It was here that the war ended for him. Don walked under a large Banyan tree, where he pulled out his maps and was getting on the radio to talk to HQ. Don figured the Japanese sniper hiding in the tree above him waited to see who the officer was and then shot Don three times in the arm and abdomen. The men wrapped Don in a blanket the sniper had carried, and they medevacked him out. Don spent the next twenty-six months in a series of hospitals and underwent six surgeries. While he eventually regained the use of his hand, he never regained the feeling in it.

Many things from the war stayed with Don the rest of his life. There were the physical aspects of the hearing loss and the loss of feeling in his hand. He also suffers from what we now know as PTSD, and a number of times he actually attacked his wife in the middle of the night during nightmare flashbacks. It was sixty years later when he was interviewed by the local newspaper that he says the ghosts finally went away. In the interview he got everything off his chest—things he had never talked about before. His wife learned much for the first time by reading that article. Don kept the sniper's blanket he was wrapped in for many years until his wife felt it was time to throw it out. In a shadow box is a pair of gloves, a briefcase, and a pack of cigarettes that his men took off the sniper and gave to him. The most important thing that stayed with Don, however, was what that Kentucky colonel said to him. He would use that philosophy to have a wonderful life, raising a wonderful and close family and becoming very successful in business.

Don Draxler

Don and his father

Credit for the Home Front

Like most Americans, when they first heard the news, sixteen-year-old Kansas farm boy Gilbert ("Gib") Dunning's first question was, "Where is Pearl Harbor?" He was too young and knew it would be a couple of years before he could get involved, if the war was still going on then. Until that time came, he did his part in something he praises highly: the efforts on the home front, which played a very important role in winning the war.

When Gib turned eighteen, he enlisted in the Army Air Corps. He shipped off to Biloxi, Mississippi, for basic training. Toward the end of training, he got sick and spent a couple of nights in the base hospital. When he returned to the barracks, all his fellow trainees, including a good friend, were gone. His friend had been sent to gunnery school and then off to Europe in a bomber. They kept in touch, and the final letter he received from his friend said he had completed all but the last of his required thirty-five missions. He was killed on that last mission. Gib has always wondered what diverted him from that same course.

Gib trained in a B-29, which he calls the Cadillac of the bombers. Unlike the B-17 or the B-24 he also trained in, the B-29 was comfortable, warm, and pressurized. Its technology was ahead of its time. Gib sat in the top turret, where he had a 360-degree view and could control all the guns on the plane. The B-29 was the plane that played a major role in the Pacific and was the model used to drop the atomic bombs on Japan, ending the war.

Gib was stationed in Tampa, Florida, when the war ended. He reenlisted and was sent to the Pacific with the 20th Air Force. He was based in Guam and flew all over the Pacific, taking trips to Manila, Tokyo, and Okinawa. During this time he also sat in on the famous military trial of Japanese officers and enlisted men accused of beheading and cannibalizing captured American Navy pilots. On a flight that was ferrying planes back to the States, he and his crew flew twenty-one hours nonstop between Guam and Hawaii. What he remembers most about that trip is coming out of a rain squall and seeing a serene 360-degree rainbow, the shadow of his plane in the middle of it.

Gib was discharged in 1947, and after working a couple of jobs, he purchased and ran a filling station for a number of years. He capped it all off with a successful real estate career. He and his wife raised three children. In 2000, using only a telephone, he successfully tracked down all but one of his original crew members, after fifty-five years, for a ceremony at the opening of a B-29 memorial located in Great Bend, Kansas. A plaque with his crew members' names on it is part of that memorial.

Throughout our discussion of his experiences, Gib kept coming back to the efforts of the home front and the unity of the country at that time. Gib still becomes emotional about this subject. "The country united as one. Its efforts on the home front were simply amazing. The home front is one of the major reasons why we won the war," Gib says as he begins to choke up.

Gilbert Dunning

Sweetheart Saved Him

George Fender might have physically been in the middle of the war in the Pacific, but his mind was constantly on Colorado. More specifically, on a beautiful seventeen-year-old girl named Dorothy Koenig in Colorado.

George had no connections to Colorado until the war broke out. Raised by his aunt, uncle, and grandmother, he grew up outside Pittsburgh, Pennsylvania. As a young kid, he used to sneak into the Pittsburgh Pirates' stadium. He eventually got to know the players and grounds crew and soon landed a job with that crew. A highlight at age twelve was meeting Babe Ruth, with whom he sat and talked for seven innings.

When the war broke out, George gave up college and a promising college football career to enlist in the Army Air Corps. He was sent by the Corps for schooling at Colorado A&M (CSU). It was there that Dorothy first caught his eye when she served him at the Aggies' café. They soon started dating and fell in love. When it was time for him to leave, he told her that if he made it back, he would marry her. She promised she would wait for him.

George moved on to Mississippi and then Florida for training as an engineer/waist gunner on a B-24 bomber. In Florida he was in a crash landing that put him in the hospital for forty days. In California he formed up in a crew and became part of the 307th Bomber Group (Long Rangers) of the 13th Air Force. They shipped out to the Pacific, where they set up at a primitive jungle base on Morotai Island. The Japanese bombed them every day.

Altogether George flew forty-nine missions. He was credited with shooting down three Japanese airplanes, and his plane was credited with sinking a Japanese destroyer. On one of his missions he was injured when he was hit by a piece of flak, and he received the Purple

Heart. On his thirty-second mission, his plane was hit, and the crew was forced to bail out. Living off the land and with help from local guerilla fighters, they managed to elude the Japanese in the jungle for the next thirty days before being rescued. Because of this experience, he could have gone home. Even if he hadn't been shot down, he was only three missions away from the mandatory thirty missions, but George instead volunteered for another seventeen missions!

Through all of this, Dorothy was always on his mind. "I constantly looked at her picture that she had sent me. We wrote each other every chance we got. She is why I made it back from the war," George says, his voice trailing off. After completing his forty-ninth mission, he had a feeling he wouldn't survive a fiftieth and finally decided it was time to go home to his Dorothy.

George and Dorothy have now been married for sixty-six years, and they have two children, four grandchildren, and one great-grandchild. George got his degree, taught for three years, worked for Conoco for seven years, had an interesting deskunking business, and topped it all off with a twenty-three-year real estate career.

George and Dorothy are inseparable and seldom apart. George often thinks about the people with whom he served, the friends he lost in the war, and especially about his crew. "A day doesn't go by that I don't think about my crew," he says.

George Fender and his Dorothy

Proud Marine

Dexter Greer was a perfect example of a proud Marine. He exemplified why the Corps is so special and why one is forever a Marine.

Dexter enlisted in the Marines in 1942, mostly because the Lee brothers in the neighborhood were Marines. He arrived at boot camp on Parris Island, where right away he encountered his drill sergeant—a tough, tough Marine by the name of Houpt. Dexter and Sgt. Houpt clashed constantly during boot camp, and initially Dex and the other men hated him. Those feelings completely reversed by the end of boot camp, however, and out of respect for Houpt the men asked whether he would ship out with them. He agreed. The unit shipped out for the Pacific as the 13th Replacement Battalion. They made stops in New Caledonia, Pearl Harbor (where, staring at the sunken fleet still on the harbor floor, Dex wondered if they could possibly win the war), the Samoan Islands, and finally New Zealand, for additional training.

While in New Zealand, Dex was taken in by a local family, the Richardsons. He soon realized that they were feeding him with their slim rations, so he always tried to arrive with a jar of marmalade, a can of Spam, or whatever he could find on the base to bring them. Mrs. Richardson treated him like a son and threatened to write his mother about his evening activities when he came in drunk one night. It is said she had a breakdown when she heard later that he was wounded.

After training in New Zealand, Dex and his unit left to fight in their first invasion, the first of four in which he would participate. He was part of the third wave to land at Tarawa, where the invasion wasn't going well. It would turn out to be one of the costliest battles of the war. Trapped at the seawall, a lieutenant told the troops that they were sitting in a killing field and had to move. He, along with a group of twenty-five, which included Dex, made a run for it across the wide-open airfield to the other side of the island. The lieutenant and nine others didn't make it. Once settled in as best they could, it was a long night for the survivors, who were vastly outnumbered. All night long the Japanese tried to engage them in a shouting match, yelling things like, "Betty Gable is a whore!" and "Babe Ruth's records are all lies!" Dex and the other Marines yelled back until Houpt grew angry and told them to shut up and not give away their positions. The next morning additional backup arrived.

The next invasion was Saipan. Dex remembers it as an excellent landing, where they never even got their feet wet. It was here, however that he was wounded, taking a shrapnel wound in the left arm. His best buddy, a Creede Indian from Oklahoma whom they called Chief, was tending to Dex's wound when he too was wounded by a sniper. Back at the field hospital, they were both told they would be evacuated off the island. They both said no, they wouldn't, and instead got patched up and against orders returned to their unit. During this time in Saipan, Dex went with Chief, who was a skilled hunter, on his nightly impromptu recon missions into no man's land. He said Chief acquired quite a collection of gold teeth, pulling them from the Japanese he killed. They would remain close friends the rest of their lives.

After a break in Hawaii, it was time for the invasion of Tinian. Once again it was a relatively easy landing. It turned out, however, to be the hardest of all of Dex's wartime experiences. It was here that he lost his beloved Sgt. Houpt. The man who Dex believed was one of the best Marines he ever knew and who believed his sole job was to keep Marines alive—and was damn good at doing that—was himself shot and killed by a sniper. He died in Dex's arms. His death profoundly affected Dex for the rest of his life.

Dex's last invasion was Okinawa. His unit was only there for two weeks. They were badly beaten up from all their previous fighting and really no longer able to defend themselves, so they were taken off the island. They were sent back to Saipan to rest and regroup. They were training for the invasion of the Japanese homeland when the atomic bombs were dropped, and the war ended. Right away they were sent to Japan as part of the occupation forces, and they landed in Nagasaki. Less than two weeks after the bomb was dropped, Dex posed for a picture at ground zero!

Dex returned home after the war, spending a couple of months in the hospital trying to save his arm. At one point doctors told him if it wasn't better in twenty-four hours, they would amputate. Fortunately an old doctor from WWI took a look at it, said he wanted to try something, and was able to save it. Although functional, his arm would give him trouble for the rest of his life.

Dex was very proud of his service, his Marines, and his country, and in his later years he gave talks to school groups, new recruits, and whoever else asked him to speak about his experiences. Unable to get city support, he also spearheaded a campaign to finance a large granite memorial in the Bradford section of his hometown of Haverhill, Massachusetts, honoring all those who served. He was a proud Marine from the day he took the oath until the day he was laid to rest with military honors.

Dexter Greer

Returning to Find Peace

As Daryl Haerther tours Okinawa, what he sees is vastly different from what he remembers the last time he was on the island. The vegetation is now lush and green, the buildings and parks well kept. It is a peaceful place. As he stands on the slope, now a golf course, where a machine gunner once had him pinned down for hours, he remembers a time when this island wasn't so peaceful—where, in fact, it was hell on earth.

The invasion of Okinawa started on April 1, 1945. Daryl arrived three weeks later as a replacement for Co. A, 383rd Infantry Regiment of the 96th Infantry Division. The landscape was stark, void of most vegetation. Immediately it was baptism by fire. While they were hiking to the front lines, a Japanese mortar called a "Boxcar" came flying toward him. It left a crater in the ground ten foot deep and twenty feet wide. To this day Daryl still hits the ground at the sound of loud noises.

After he arrived at the front lines, his commander asked whether he would volunteer to go back to the field hospital for medical training. With so many casualties (his company would incur nearly a 200 percent casualty rate, meaning that the soldiers sent to replace those killed or injured were themselves killed or injured), they were short of medics. With just two days of training, Daryl now acted as a medic, though he still carried a weapon.

Daryl spent the next two months in a foxhole. He and his foxhole mate took turns keeping watch, while the other tried to grab some sleep. They lived on rations, and only once during this time did they ever have a hot meal. When the rainy season came, they lived in mud and used their helmets to bail out their foxhole. Like almost everyone else, Daryl suffered from jungle rot, a terrible skin rash.

The fighting was fierce, with their success in moving the front line measured in yards. But according to Daryl, it was nighttime that was the worst. The Japanese constantly tried to infiltrate their positions. They put on American helmets to make their silhouettes look American and became good at saying such things as "Don't shoot, Joe. It's me." Daryl remembers one time when a group of Japanese soldiers posing as civilians approached with white flags. All of a sudden the front row bent over, machine guns strapped to their backs, and the men behind them started firing the guns. "You just couldn't ever let your guard down," Daryl says.

Daryl carries many sad memories of that island. One of the saddest memories is one that should have been happy. He received word from back home that someone from his hometown in Iowa was on the island. One day Daryl went to find him, only to discover that his friend had been killed the day before.

Daryl's time on the front lines came to an end when, while carrying a stretcher, he was hit in the arm and back with shrapnel, and his commanding officer was killed. Evacuated to the beach hospital, he still wasn't safe. During a kamikaze attack, a piece of flak tore through the hospital tent and killed the man lying next to him. Daryl was evacuated to Guam and eventually to Saipan, where he waited to rejoin his unit after the war ended. There was no celebration, just a huge sigh of relief. Had the war continued, and they had gone on to invade the Japanese homeland, it would have been Okinawa a thousand times over. Daryl received the Purple Heart and was awarded the Bronze Star for bravery.

Okinawa today is a very beautiful place, and the Okinawans are a polite and friendly people. They erected a beautiful memorial park named the Cornerstone of Peace, which has the names of all who were killed engraved on walls of polished granite. This includes American and Japanese military personnel as well as residents of Okinawa, which lost one third of its population during the battle. Daryl returned to Okinawa with his wife Betty for the fiftieth anniversary of the battle and again in 2001 with Betty and their daughters and sons-in-law. Fortunately for Daryl's family, their only memories of the island are ones of beauty and peace.

Daryl Haerther

Deep Service

In the murky, cold waters off the Rhode Island coast, George Hekowczyk labored in total darkness. Working purely by his sense of touch, he found what he was looking for and attached the cable. Another torpedo was retrieved.

Underwater diving in 1942 consisted of heavy diving helmets and life support hoses dangling from the surface. Diving was still in its infancy. So was George, as he was still just a teenager.

George enlisted in the Navy a month after Pearl Harbor was bombed. Born and raised in Webster, Massachusetts, he shipped out not too far from home to Providence, Rhode Island. He got no basic training and instead was immediately assigned to a secret base on islands off the coast. He was now part of a unique, seldom heard of, and very dangerous diving unit at a torpedo testing center.

Military supplies and equipment were in short supply when the war broke out. America was still recovering from the Great Depression, and nothing could be wasted, including torpedoes. At the base, every torpedo was tested before being sent out to ships, planes, or submarines. The torpedoes were tested during the day, and at night the dive crews went out and retrieved each one.

Being the "kid" on the crew, George was initially part of surface support. "One day, out of the blue, someone said, 'Ski [his nickname], get dressed, you're going down,'" George remembers. They put him through a variety of situations to see if he could take it, mentally. A number of dives later, George was now officially a diver.

The process of retrieving the torpedoes involved determining their rough location and sending down a diver. Using a weight on a rope or a metal rod, the diver would probe around in the deep mud until he hit something solid. A two-and-a-half-inch fire hose was then sent down, and forced air would start blowing everything away from the torpedo. "You were digging, but it was more like everything was suspended in the water. You were encased in a Jell-O-like substance while you worked," George explains. "You then felt along the torpedo until you found the correct area and attached a cable to it."

After each dive George spent time in the decompression chamber to ensure that he wouldn't get the bends—an extremely painful and potentially fatal condition that can develop in response to rapid changes in pressure. One time George developed the bends after retiring to his bunk for the night. He began screaming from the extreme pain caused by nitrogen being released into his joints and muscles. The older divers realized what was wrong and put him in the chamber, where he spent eleven hours. George had another diving accident when he fell off an underwater cliff and slammed his face into his diving helmet.

Once war production got up to full speed, and there were now plenty of torpedoes, George was transferred to the destroyer escort *Charles E. Brannon*. The *Brannon* sailed throughout the Pacific, primarily as a submarine hunter, and George crossed the equator thirteen times. Although he had no formal navy training, he took on many responsibilities on the ship in addition to his diving work. Being given a task with little or no training and then excelling at it is a common thread, both in George's military life and later in his civilian life.

Along with the memories, George has physical reminders of his service. Years later, he required a number of surgeries to correct the injuries he sustained in that diving accident. His knees still cause him pain as a result of getting the bends and are prone to giving out from time to time. He also has hearing issues caused by the constant changes in pressure he endured during all his years of service. George is extremely proud of his service, though, and has no regrets.

George Hekowczyk

Interesting Life

Loyd Johnson is looking back over his life. One chapter in this life was his time in the Navy during World War II. As is the rest of his life, his wartime experiences were truly fascinating.

Loyd was born and raised in Paynesville, Minnesota. He grew up on one of the many lakes in the region, and it was an idyllic life for a boy. Pearl Harbor was bombed in December of his senior year in high school, and, like everyone else his age, he assumed he would eventually be involved in the war. After he graduated, however, he had the opportunity to go to California and work for Lockheed Aircraft. "As I look back now on that experience at Lockheed, I am amazed at the amount of responsibility they gave me as an eighteen-year-old," he says.

Uncle Sam eventually came calling, and Loyd received his draft notice. His boss offered to get him a deferment, as he was in a defense-based industry, but Loyd declined and said he would serve. He attended boot camp in San Diego and then went to San Francisco, where he boarded a ship heading to the Pacific.

Arriving in Hawaii, Loyd was assigned to the personnel department of the submarine base there. He helped handle the files of the 10,000 personnel on the base, long before computers existed to assist with such a monumental task. He soon had the opportunity to become the aide to the commander responsible for all the torpedoes in the Pacific Fleet. This position gave him a behind-the-scenes, top-secret view of the war. It also necessitated a background clearance check by the FBI, and the requirement that he report all his movements to the FBI whenever he left the base. He met top admirals such as Nimitz and Halsey and sat in on their meetings as they planned campaigns and discussed the war. He knew about all the battles and invasions before they happened. Another responsibility he had was reading and processing all the submarine logs when the subs came back to the base.

Loyd remembers a massive explosion at Pearl Harbor in 1944. The harbor was the staging area for an upcoming island invasion. There were hundreds of ships docked there, including a number of ammunitions ships and fuel ships. Suddenly one of the ammunition ships blew up, which set off a chain reaction among the other vessels. It has been called the Second Pearl Harbor Disaster. "I am baffled that you look at history books and find very little written about it," Loyd says.

Loyd was always a man of faith, but a number of personal experiences in the service further strengthened his faith. After he returned home from the war, Loyd started down a path that would lead into the ministry and a forty-year career as a pastor in churches throughout the Midwest. After retiring, he spent another fifteen years in an international faith and humanitarian organization. This took him to twenty-three different countries, and in the course of these travels, he crossed the Atlantic over fifty times. A truly fascinating life to date.

Loyd Johnson

Just a Country Boy

Bob Kelley is a self-proclaimed country boy. Having grown up on a farm in Medina, Ohio, he has never cared much for city life. That country life he so loves was interrupted, though, when the Army plucked him away from it.

Being away from home for the first time was a big change, but army life was an even bigger change. He requested a transfer to the Army Air Corps, where he got into the cadet program and received his wings flying multiengine planes. While still in advanced training, Bob and some buddies went to dinner and a movie one night. When they returned to base, it was completely deserted. Everyone had been rushed to Europe, as the Battle of the Bulge had started. Left behind, Bob and his buddies became trainers when the new round of cadets came to the base.

While Bob was training cadets, there was an incident that nearly became tragic but instead turned into a heartwarming memory for him. He was leading a group of cadets on a cross-country training flight when they ran into a snowstorm. The heavy snow was starting to pull the planes down. Bob flew by a water tower and then saw a school and a large field, where he safely brought all the planes down. Attracted by all the activity, people starting appearing from everywhere. The townspeople brought the fliers into the school, made up beds for them, brought in home-cooked meals, including cookies and desserts, and just plain pampered them. “They treated us like kings,” Bob recalls fondly. The next morning the weather broke, and they were able to return to the base.

Bob eventually got his overseas orders and shipped off to New Guinea. From there he started island-hopping north to front-line jungle bases, first with the 5th Air Force, then with the 550th Night Fighter Squadron of the 13th Air Force. Bob received seven battle stars. His missions included softening beaches for invading Marines, providing air cover for the Navy, and searching out Japanese ships.

He was in charge of the squadron and getting them back home safely—a lot of responsibility on the shoulders of a twenty-year-old.

Bob doesn't like to think of the bad times associated with war, but there were fun times as well, which make him laugh. Like someone's pet monkey, who pestered everyone in the camp, or the time he and some buddies checked out planes and flew to another island to see Bob Hope. That incident got him in trouble for a month, with extra flying duty.

He finally had enough points to come home, but he was still far from being out of danger. He was angry when he was bumped from a ship heading home, only to find out later that it hit a mine and sank. The ship he did get on broke down at sea, and they floated for days while repairs were being made, eventually running out of food and water.

Once home, Bob wanted to continue to fly and was hired by UPS flying freight. He was soon grounded, though, when he flunked the physical because of an ear injury he had sustained during a Japanese bombing of his base. He then went to work at his dad's manufacturing business, building it up and eventually selling it. He ultimately moved west and had a successful career with a log home manufacturer. After all he has seen and done in his life, the country has always remained in Bob's blood, and he retired in a beautiful log home nestled in the foothills of the Rocky Mountains.

Bob Kelley

From Playboy to Warrior

Ken Killilea was a self-professed playboy before the war. His parents were divorced, and his dad gave him a car and a nice allowance, so he just played around, with no real direction. Then, on December 7, Japan attacked Pearl Harbor, and Ken went down to enlist in the Marines on December 8. When he went to enlist, however, he was told that he was too skinny and didn't meet the minimum weight requirement for the Marines. So he checked himself into the YMCA, where he says they have a reputation for making musclemen out of weaklings. He began working out and living off milkshakes until the summer, when he had finally gained enough weight and chest circumference to join up.

Once enlisted, he was off to Parris Island for boot camp and the rude awakening brought on by the Marines' rigorous training. Ken says their drill sergeant took them from flesh and hair and broke them down to nothing but a pile of clay, then turned around and molded them into Marines. He says he now looks back on the process with humor. When asked if he also looks back with admiration for that drill sergeant, he responds, "No, I still don't like him." Toward the end of training, the sergeant said, "You won't be long in the States. Between here and Tokyo, 70 percent of you will be killed!" With a teenage sense of invincibility, Ken looked at the guys all around him and said to himself, "You poor bastards."

With boot camp behind him and having been transformed into a strong Marine, Ken started that journey with the ultimate goal of Tokyo. He was now part of the 4th Marine Division, which was the first division to go directly from the States right into battle—the invasion of the Marshall Islands, where he said they acted like John Wayne walking onto the beach, shooting their machine guns from their hips. They soon learned that this wasn't like training, however, since the Japanese were shooting back. He would participate in five island invasions, each getting progressively worse as they approached Japan. During the invasion of Saipan, he remembers wearing the same clothes without a shower for fifty-seven days. He landed with green skivvies on, and when he finally left the island they were white, because salt had eaten away the dye. He also remembers watching Japanese soldiers and civilians jumping off the cliffs rather than being taken prisoner. When they caught someone before he could jump, they asked him why. He said everyone had been told that to get into the Marines, one had to kill either his father or a brother. If that was what a Marine would do to his own family, they were afraid of what would happen to them if they were captured.

Ken would never make it all the way to the end of the war in the Marines. During the invasion of Iwo Jima, Ken and the other eight members of his unit were in a shell crater when a shell exploded above them. Ken and his buddy were lying on their sides, facing each other, and they were both badly injured, riddled with shrapnel on their exposed sides. The other seven Marines in his unit were killed. Ken said there was nothing recognizable left of those seven, and he and his buddy had to lie among the flesh and blood of their remains for five hours before medics could get to them. As they were evacuated, trying to reach safety and medical attention, they came under another artillery barrage, and Ken's buddy died en route. Ken isn't sure whether he was hit again in the barrage or died of shock. Ken, lying out in the open on a gurney, was the only survivor of the nine-man unit.

He would spend the next six months recovering in a series of hospitals. Like many of his fellow veterans, once he was discharged, he just wanted to move on and forget everything. "I got out on September 7 and was married on September 9. I just wanted to get on with life and put what happened behind me. I never thought about it or talked about it," he says. In fact, years later his son approached him and told him that he needed to go down to the costume shop to get a military uniform for a school play. Ken said he could use his. His son was stunned. He had no idea Ken had served in the military and did not know his incredible story!

Ken Killilea

Multiple Love Affairs

Wayne Leroy has two had life-long loves—Loretta and airplanes.

His first love affair started when he was eight years old, and a barnstormer landed in the field of the next farm over. A ride up in that plane, and he was hooked. After he graduated from high school, he went into nearby Wichita and applied for a job at the Boeing Aircraft plant. He was promptly hired and started out working on the Stearman trainer. He began working his way up in the company and was soon involved with the development of the B-29. When the war broke out, Boeing wouldn't release him for service because of his role in the company, and he was deferred until the plane was fully developed and well into production.

When Boeing finally released him, Wayne enlisted in the Army Air Corps and began what was a historically unique role in World War II. He was assigned to the 882nd Bomb Squad of the 500th Bomb Group stationed in Saipan. He not only helped design and then built the B-29, he was now flying missions in one as the top turret gunner! Altogether he flew twenty-eight missions. It was during one of these missions that his unique knowledge of the plane came in handy. As he was returning from a bombing mission to Japan, both engines on the right side of the plane went out. The pilot came over the intercom to say that they were unable to transfer the fuel from that side to the left side and that the crew should prepare to ditch the plane in the ocean, as they would soon run out of fuel. Wayne asked whether he could come down and take a look at things. Sitting in the engineer's seat, he tried the same procedure and was also unable to transfer the fuel. He then remembered a different way they did it back at the plant. This was successful, and they landed back at the base with plenty of fuel to spare. Once they were on the ground, the pilot came up to him, shook his hand, and told Wayne that if it weren't for him, the crew would have been floating in rafts in the middle of the Pacific Ocean.

His knowledge was called upon on the ground as well. While most crews rested between missions, Wayne spent most of his free time helping out the ground maintenance crews on the base with various mechanical issues.

The base on Saipan was right across the water from another B-29 base on Tinian. Wayne didn't know it at the time, but he was witnessing history. Everyone had binoculars and was watching a strange event on Tinian. A B-29 was completely encircled by MPs, but what was strange about it was that they were all facing outward from the plane. The next day Wayne and the crew were sitting in their plane on the tarmac ready to leave on another mission to Japan when word came from the tower to abort the mission . . . the atomic bomb had been dropped.

Wayne remained on Saipan for six months after the war ended until he had enough points to return home to his other love, his wife Loretta, who was his high school sweetheart. Wayne had left Loretta and a newborn daughter for the Pacific Theater, and it was two years before he saw them again. He returned home on a Thursday, and by the following Monday he was back to work at his old job at Boeing, where he went on to have a very fulfilling thirty-six-year career. He now had all his loves together. These loves would double to include not only Loretta and his aviation career, but also his infant daughter and soon another.

He and Loretta shared almost sixty-six years of blissful marriage before she passed away. "The only girl I ever dated my entire life," Wayne says with pride.

Wayne Leroy

Separation

David Landers was in his freshman year at the University of Wyoming when Pearl Harbor was bombed. A few months later he enlisted, choosing the Army Air Corps because he wanted to fly. They told him they would defer his enlistment until he graduated from college, but it didn't work out that way, as he was called up the following year.

David was sent to Missouri for basic training and schooling. He was then transferred to California for flight school. Training in single engine planes, he soon discovered that he got sick while doing loops and rolls, and the base doctors decided to wash him out of the program. Still very much wanting to fly, however, David requested and received a transfer to fly multiengine bombers.

The transfer brought him to the air base in La Junta, Colorado, to train with the B-25 bomber. Since he was now closer to Wyoming, his fiancée, Nancy, a cute coed David had met at a mixer on their first day of school, joined him, and they were married in Pueblo. She stayed in Colorado with him until he received his orders to go overseas.

David shipped off for the Pacific with the 405th Bomb Squad, 38th Bomber Group of the 5th Air Force, leaving behind a pregnant Nancy. Because of the slow communications at that time, it was two months after the birth of his child that he learned he was the father of a baby girl. It was nine months before he was actually able to see and hold his daughter.

David first landed in New Guinea and then moved up to the Philippines before traveling on to Okinawa, where he was based. Outside of a mission to Borneo, he flew all his twelve missions over the Sea of Japan. These missions were designed to take out Japanese cargo and supply ships. They served a dual purpose—to prevent supplies from getting to Japan, but also to train the airman for their part in the planned invasion of the Japanese homeland.

David's plane was equipped with fourteen forward guns, rockets, and bombs, and he flew it no more than fifty feet off the surface of the water. In his arsenal were skip bombs, which were dropped and which then bounced into the ships. This maneuver had to be timed very precisely, or David risked blowing off the tail of his plane.

In August 1945, the atomic bombs were dropped, and Japan surrendered. Shortly after that, David was assigned the task of flying a colonel and some nurses up to Korea. En route, they made numerous low-level passes over Hiroshima and Nagasaki and got a bird's eye view of the destruction. He was awed by the complete destruction caused by these bombs. On the return flight, low on fuel and unable to return to Seoul or land in Japan because of the weather, David's only choice was to try to make it as close as possible to Okinawa and land in the sea. "The backup bomb bay tanks on all planes had been ordered emptied at the war's end, but we checked them, and by the grace of the Lord there was enough fuel in them to make it," David says.

Following a short time in Japan, David returned home to Nancy and their daughter, Janet. He laughs as he looks at a picture of him holding Janet. The baby has her arms around Nancy's neck. "She wanted no part of this stranger," David says with a chuckle.

Nancy, Janet and Dave

Fighting Fear

One of the many things Clarence ("Mac") Matheny wondered about when he headed off to war was how he would handle fear.

What occupied his mind before that, however, was whether he would even get into the service. Prior to the start of the war, with war clouds on the horizon, Mac had tried to enlist. He badly wanted to fly and tried to get into the Marines, the Navy, and the Army Air Corps. All turned him down because he is color-blind. Instead he went to trade school and got a job in the aircraft industry.

His draft notice eventually came after the war had started, and after a couple of deferments because he was in a war-related industry, he declined another deferment and headed off to the Army. After boot camp, the Army sent him to school to learn how to maintain and repair electronic equipment. "No one would take me when I tried to enlist because I am color-blind. I get drafted, and they put me in a situation where I deal with multicolored wires!" Mac says with a chuckle. "That's the Army for you. Send you off to baker's school to become a truck driver."

After electronics school, Mac started out on what would be an eye-opening adventure for this Missouri farm boy. On the West Coast he loaded onto a ship that first made a stop in Australia. Its next stop was Bombay, India, where Mac boarded a train, ultimately serving at a number of radar installations in India and Burma as part of the 559th Signal Aircraft Warning Battalion, which was attached to the 10th Air Force.

What he was seeing and experiencing was astonishing to him: the incredible poverty in India, the headhunter tribes in Burma with their trophies on poles, and the very difficult and unfamiliar conditions in which he lived in the jungle. It would be in the jungles of Burma where Mac faced fear.

One night while out on patrol, he got separated from his unit. It was pitch-black, but somehow he made it back to where they were bivouacked. Sitting there alone, he began to hear rustling in the eight-foot-high buffalo grass around him. All night long he sat there listening to the sounds while gripping his carbine and his knife, expecting to be attacked by the Japanese at any moment. "My heart was pounding so hard, it felt like it was going to pop out of my ears," Mac remembers. His unit finally returned, and he was now safe. An inspection of the grass at daylight revealed that the night sounds had been made by a pack of jackals.

When the war finally ended, Howard's unit left Burma and waited in India for a ship home. They went up through the Suez Canal and the Mediterranean Sea and then across the Atlantic to New York. With this final segment of his journey home, he had now completely circumnavigated the globe. Talking about seeing the Statue of Liberty still brings tears to Mac's eyes. "You looked at her, and you realized you had been away fighting to protect her," Mac said.

Mac returned to the Midwest and worked for a number of years in the oil fields. Then he became an iron worker, which eventually led him to open his own business installing large doors on such structures as aircraft hangars. He and his wife, Lola, have been married for more than sixty years, and they have three children and five grandchildren.

His war experiences answered his question about how he would handle fear. "Ever since that night in the jungle, I have never been afraid of anything," Mac says.

Clarence Matheny

Decaying Hopes

The horror that Don Norbie experienced at dusk off the coast of Tarawa while at the helm of the USS *Mobile* has haunted him his entire life.

Prior to that evening, life was pretty good. Don had joined the Navy and had gone through quartermaster school. In the Army, quartermaster means supply. In the Navy, it means navigation. It was a fascinating and challenging position, and Don loved the work. He particularly enjoyed steering the ship. The primary mission of the *Mobile*, a cruiser, was to support the various island invasions in the South Pacific as US forces worked their way toward Japan.

This particular mission involved supporting the invasion of Tarawa. The *Mobile* sailed in a continuous motion up and down the coast and helped soften the beach with shells. The landing invasion itself was not going well. When the invasion was planned, the barrier reefs surrounding the island had been miscalculated. Landing craft got caught up on the reefs or were sunk by them, hundreds of feet out from the beaches. Forced to wade in, the Marines were exposed in the water and were being cut down by the hundreds. If they were lucky enough to make it to the beach, they found that it was too narrow for everyone to take cover. During the fighting in the seventy-six- hour battle to capture an island the size of Central Park, nearly 1,000 Marines were killed, 2,400 were wounded, and 90 of the 125 landing craft were lost.

Back out at sea, the *Mobile* began another sweep of the coast. Don was now on duty at his general quarters, steering the ship. As they cruised down the coast, they came across a horrible sight, which at first they mistook as a debris field. As they got closer, though, they realized that ahead of them were hundreds of bodies floating in the water, bloated and disfigured by the tropical heat. The tide had taken out to sea those slaughtered in the lagoon earlier that day. What seared this vision further into Don's memory was what the captain said next: "Try not to run over them, as they are our boys."

In 1975, more than thirty years later, Don would pen a poem about that experience, which he has never been able to forget.

Decaying Hopes

Gray ships roll gently
Decks piled high
With spent shell casings,
Angry guns silent.
Standing my watch,
I scan the sea,
Bloated bags
Of human flesh,
Bursting taut skin,
Bob on the heaving bosom
Of an anguished sea.
Decaying hopes . . .
Brave young men
Hit that beach,
Facing a storm of steel and fire
That blasted them into the sea.

Budding dreams—
A business, a wife's caress, laughing children,
A life lived full—
Rot,
Fueled by tropic sun . . .
A man vomits,
And I cling to my God.

Donald L. Norbie

Don Norbie

Stretched

The story of Jim Olstad's service in World War II is one of incredible sacrifice, and it shows how resilient humans can be when stretched to the limits.

Jim enlisted in the Army in the spring of 1941. He was one of the first members of the 46th Construction Engineers Battalion (Steel Spike), a World War I unit that was being reactivated. A week after Pearl Harbor, the 46th took off for the Pacific. They initially headed for the Philippines, but when it fell to the Japanese, the ship turned toward Australia. With the war so new and the Army not ramped up, procedures and logistics were not in place yet. There was not enough food on the ship during this forty-two-day trip, and the men were starving. "I remember when someone was lucky to have an orange or an apple, someone else would follow behind and pick up the peel or core and eat it," Jim recalls.

That trip was representative of the rest of Jim's time overseas. More often than not his unit was given little support and left to its own devices to survive.

After landing in Melbourne, where the Salvation Army fed them, they worked their way up to northern Australia and began to do what they were sent to do—build air bases. From Australia they shipped to New Guinea and began island-hopping as the war moved toward Japan. Each new location required hacking a base out of the jungle. Conditions were very primitive and isolated. They were perpetually wet and dirty. Bugs were constantly biting them, and they were always having to deal with big jungle rats and eighteen-foot snakes. Food and gas containers quickly rusted out. Often short of supplies, they lived off the land. They ate wild yams, melons, and bananas. They killed wild boar for meat. These conditions required them to invent and improvise. It would be fifteen months before Jim got a letter to his folks. While they worked to build these bases, they were given no protection. "We were sitting ducks," Jim remembers. "We set up machine guns along the area we were working in. If we came under attack, we jumped off the grader or tractor and ran to the nearest gun to operate it."

They worked their way up to the Philippines, where Jim was in the second wave during the invasion of Leyte. A couple of days later, after everything was secured, he was walking along the beach when he came upon men setting up cameras. He witnessed the famous scene of Gen. Douglas MacArthur coming ashore.

It was in the Philippines that Jim finally accumulated enough points to come home. His parents were in shock when they saw him. Despite his hearty Norwegian stock, the jungle had left him just a shell of a man. Wracked with malaria and yellow jaundice, he weighed less than 120 pounds. It took him six months to recover.

Once recovered, he went on to a sixty-five-year career in construction. He also continued to use the skills he developed in the jungle, coming up with—and patenting—a number of inventions.

Jim goes to all the 46th Engineers Battalion reunions; he is the last from that original unit to attend. The reunions are now attended by younger guys from more recent conflicts. He is revered by these younger members. The first thing they always ask when they check in is, "Is Jim here again this year?"

Jim Olstad (l)

Okie Goes to Sea

The first question you want to ask Bob O'Rourke is, "How did an Okie wind up in the Navy?" The idea was put into his mind by his dad, a brick mason by trade, who was hit hard by the Great Depression. He told Bob that he should join the Navy when he grew up, as it provides three square meals, a bed, and job security. When Bob graduated from high school at seventeen, the war was raging, and he did just that, with the idea that he would make it his career.

After boot camp and additional training in electrical, Bob shipped out to the Pacific. It was exciting going off to the unknown—and unnerving as well. No sooner did they pass under the Golden Gate Bridge when Tokyo Rose, a propaganda DJ for the Japanese government, came over the air, warning that his transport ship was soon going to be blown out of the water. The ship made it to Hawaii without incident, however, and from there, Bob continued on to New Guinea.

While in New Guinea at a receiving station awaiting assignment, Bob drew guard duty.

Japanese soldiers still held out in the jungles, and they sneaked in at night to rummage in the garbage for food. "Looking back, at that age I would probably have shot them. I feel fortunate that I never had to. Now, I probably would point them in the right direction. They were harmless and just hungry," Bob recalls.

The Philippines had recently been liberated, and Bob was assigned to the Seabees, the nickname for the Navy's construction battalions, helping to build and maintain an air base for the Army Air Corps on the island of Samar. Since the base was very isolated, it initially seemed like Shangri-La: the setting was beautiful, and the sailors and natives got along well. Bob once again came across some more garbage divers looking for food. This time, however, the scavengers were native children. For the next two years, Bob took this group of six hungry boys under his wing, looking after them and making sure they had plenty to eat. He still gets emotional when he thinks of the day he shipped out and left them behind. He thinks about them to this day, wondering whatever became of their lives.

When the Japanese surrendered, Bob was transferred from the base and would spend the remainder of his service at sea. He served on a mine sweeper, a net tender, a tanker, and a land craft mechanized (LCM), sailing throughout the Pacific. Serving aboard the tanker was a particularly bad time for him. Morale onboard was extremely poor and conditions not much better. One particular mission took them to Bikini Atoll to restart a ship and bring it back to Hawaii. The US government had recently tested an atomic bomb there and wanted to study the effects on the battleship, one of many anchored around the atoll. The men spent time on the ship and then on the beach, Geiger counters buzzing the whole time. Unable to start or tow the test ship, they finally left.

His experience on the tanker ended any thoughts Bob had of making a career in the Navy. Another component to the decision involved a beautiful woman, Lou, whom had he met while home on leave. Bob left the Navy after his service was finished and used the GI Bill to go to college, obtaining multiple degrees. He found the job security his father told him to seek out in the education field. He was a teacher and counselor, and finished up with a successful twenty-two-year career as a school psychologist.

Bob O'Rourke

The Letters

Buford Plemmons can tell the story of the war and his own experiences simply by reading through the letters that he sent his wife during that time. Before he shipped out, they devised a plan of numbering the islands in the Pacific so she would know where he was. Normally, such information was censored out of homebound letters for security reasons. Buford and Lori wrote each other every day. Sixty-five years later, one of his most cherished objects is the leather suitcase full of these letters.

Buford was born on a farm in southwest Oklahoma and rode a mule or horse to a two-room schoolhouse. He was in college when Pearl Harbor was bombed. Having grown up near Fort Sill, he knew he didn't want to be in the Army, so he enlisted in the Navy. He entered the Navy's V-12 program. Before being transferred to Norfolk for seamen's training, he returned home to become engaged. After Norfolk he headed to Chicago for midshipmen's school.

Upon graduating as an ensign, he got a nine-day leave of absence before reporting to his ship. He and Lori scrambled to put together all the arrangements and get married. The couple then left together for Norfolk, where he met up with his crew and new ship, the LST *1032*. A landing ship tank (LST) was a large, flat-bottomed ship that could go right up onto the beach. It was the workhorse of the Navy during the war, delivering supplies, equipment, and personnel. After four months of fitting and training, the *1032* set sail for the Pacific.

Buford and the *1032* first saw action during the battle of Iwo Jima, delivering a contingent of the 4th Marines. The battle for the small island was fierce. Of the twenty-seven DUCWs (amphibious trucks) that the LST unloaded, only five still remained functional after the second day of battle. During the voyage to the island, Buford got to know a Marine lieutenant. They sat up on the top deck in the evening and had long conversations. The night before he went ashore, his new friend sold his watch to Buford. The next day, while unloading, the Marine's DUCW sank, and he tried to swim back to the LST. Buford watched in horror as his friend was run over and sucked under by the ship.

Buford served as the deck officer stationed at the front of the ship. This gave him a grandstand view of the horrible fighting going on, on the island. He also watched the first and then the second flag go up on Mt. Suribachi. Buford's ship next saw action at Okinawa. The operation wasn't as dangerous this time, as they delivered a Marine construction unit being brought in once the beach was deemed secure. They weren't completely out of danger, however. The skies were full of kamikazes, and the ship next to them took a direct hit from one. LST-*1032* would go on to make three trips to Japan after the war, delivering occupation troops before heading back to the States.

I thought I understood why that suitcase full of letters meant so much to Buford, as he had lost his Lori just six months earlier. But it became even clearer when I asked him how he thought he made it through that war experience. With tears streaming down his cheeks, he pointed at the suitcase and said, "My wife at home and these letters she faithfully sent me every day were my strength."

Buford and Lori

The letters

Thank *You*!

When you try to thank Don Ratschkowsky for his service to our country, he tells you that you have it all backward. It is he who is thankful for what this country gave to him; he says it gave far more than he ever gave back. One of the most important things it gave to him was his citizenship.

Don was born in Yorkton, Saskatchewan, Canada. At an early age he moved to Montana and then on to a number of towns in Idaho as the family followed his father's career in the ministry. His father finally gave up the ministry and took a job in Rochester, New York, when Don was in high school. Don left school his junior year to work and was soon drafted into the Navy.

Being in the military speeded up the process of obtaining his citizenship. Once he got it, he was able to progress from boot camp, and he went off to quartermaster school. Upon completing his training, he traveled across the States and then to the Pacific to join his ship, the USS *Requisit*e—a minesweeper—in the Philippines. As the ship's quartermaster, Don had a wide range of important responsibilities, primarily centered around navigation and visual communications. One of his favorite duties was steering the ship and teaching other sailors how to do so as well.

Don joined the ship at the tail end of the war, and they sailed around the waters of the Philippines and Okinawa, clearing out the mines. When the war came to an end, the ship headed for Japan. The waters of Japan were heavily mined, and the *Requisite* helped clear the mines so that he occupation forces could safely sail into Japan. During this duty, Don had a number of opportunities to go ashore. He remembers the Japanese at the docks waving small American flags as they came in. He was amazed by the destruction he saw but also by the ingenuity of the Japanese people: he observed Japanese cars rigged to operate by charcoal stoves because there was no gasoline.

Once the *Requisite* completed her duties, she sailed back home to the West Coast, down through the Panama Canal, and up to New York, where Don was discharged. He returned home to Rochester, and, using the veteran's accelerated school program, earned his high school diploma. He eventually joined Eastman Kodak and would go on to a thirty-two-year career there. He also met and married Marilyn, to whom he has been married for fifty-seven years.

Don says he is very grateful for how his life has turned out. Grateful for his childhood, his time in the Navy—a job that he looked forward to every day—and for his wife and family. He is also grateful to this country. "The thanks go to this country for what it did for me, rather than what I did for it," Don says. Marilyn adds, "He has always said and felt that."

Don Ratschkowsky (m)

Special Person

Thad Reed is one of the nicest people you will ever meet. He genuinely looks for the good in everyone. He speaks of everyone he has ever known in glowing terms: "So and so was such a great person" or "Those people were so wonderful." He truly loves people and no doubt is loved by everyone with whom he has crossed paths. His disposition is ideal for the medical profession.

Thad got into medicine via the Navy. He chose to join the Navy in 1938, based on stories he remembers one of his "special" grandfathers telling him as a child. His grandfather served with General Sherman in the Civil War and told stories about the brutality of that war. Thad wanted no part of that. Once in the Navy, he seriously considered medicine as a profession and went on to become a cardiologist.

Thad was serving at the Naval hospital in San Diego when Pearl Harbor was bombed. The following spring he was chosen for the team heading to New Zealand to set up a hospital for battle casualties in the South Pacific. He was taken in by a "wonderful" family that had lost a son in the African campaign. He says they treated him like a son. With so many Kiwis off to war, he taught at a medical school in his spare time.

After seven months in New Zealand, he joined the Navy hospital ship the USS *Benevolence* and sailed for Australia. From there, the ship began the journey north in support of the many island invasions. The ship usually remained about twelve miles behind the warships. During one of the Philippine invasions, the USS *California* was hit by a kamikaze, and forty-four men were killed, including eight medical corpsmen. Thad was temporarily transferred to that ship to fill in until a new contingent of corpsmen could be brought on.

Thad finally rejoined the *Benevolence*, which continued to follow the war north. During the battle of Okinawa, Thad's ship was anchored next to the USS *Pennsylvania* when it too was hit by a kamikaze.

Thad remembers helping rescue a number of people from that ship, including a young ensign who would go on to be the "great" entertainer Johnny Carson.

With the Japanese surrender, the *Benevolence* raced to Japan and was in Tokyo Harbor during the formal surrender ceremonies. While in Japan, Thad was faced with a dilemma. When the *Benevolence* first left New Zealand more than three years earlier, Thad had sought permission from the skipper to bring aboard two mascots—a dog named Skipper and a penguin named Millie. Thad was concerned about Skipper and Millie because, with the war now over, the ship's future was uncertain. He soon befriended a Japanese civilian ("one of many nice Japanese") and one day explained his situation. The problem was instantly solved, as the man's wife worked at a zoo.

Thad returned to the States and married his "dear" Ethel. They had known each other years earlier in San Diego, but the war scattered them, and they had lost touch. In a chance meeting at a church function, Ethel sat at the same table as Thad's mother, and after the two women put two and two together, his mother put Ethel and her son in contact with each other.

Thad would go on to spend twenty-four years in the Navy, serving aboard the hospital ship the USS *Repose* during the Korean War. He followed that up with a twenty-two-year career with the VA. He and Ethel would have a wonderful life together.

I feel honored and grateful to have met such an "incredible" man.

Thad Reed

Years at Sea

Alexander Rothe wondered and worried about his buddies when he heard the news about the attack on Pearl Harbor. He was on the West Coast for advanced training, and he now sat waiting to board a vessel that would take him to rejoin his ship, the USS *Ralph Talbot*, which was in Pearl Harbor.

Alex was part of a wave of Germans from Russia who came to America. He was born in Germany while his family was in transit and arrived in Colorado as an infant. At age sixteen he joined the Civilian Conservation Corps to help earn money for the family and worked at a camp in the mountains. The CCC was a national program that helped put young men to work during the Great Depression. In January 1941, he and his buddy Jake decided to join the Navy. Since he was just seventeen, he needed to have his parents sign permission papers, which they initially declined to do, with the result that he lagged behind Jake. Although they left for boot camp at different times, both he and Jake would end up on the *Ralph Talbot*.

Shortly after the attack, Alex arrived in Pearl Harbor to rejoin his ship. There was still smoking wreckage everywhere. The *Ralph Talbot*, a destroyer, had survived because the Japanese targeted the larger battleships and cruisers. Alex's ship joined up with what was left of the Pacific fleet, and they sailed to take the fight back to the Japanese. This would be the start of a long stint at sea for Alex.

He spent three years of his service aboard the *Ralph Talbot*. He handled fire control, which directed fire for the guns on the ship. He sailed throughout the Pacific, getting involved in sea battles and island invasions. During the battle of Savo Island, his ship was hit severely. With the vessel on fire and listing badly, the command was sent out to abandon ship. "I really didn't have any good choices," Alex recalls. "If I jumped over on the listing side, I was afraid the ship would roll over on me. I went over to the other side, but if I jumped there, I would have landed on the hull and broken a leg."

Luckily another command followed to try to save the ship. Using mattresses to plug the holes, they managed to save her, and she limped back for repairs.

While back in the States for a ship overhaul, Alex became sick. The Navy wanted to give him a medical discharge, but Alex insisted on going back to sea. With the *Ralph Talbot* now gone, he was assigned to another destroyer, the USS *Lewis Hancock*. He would go on to serve aboard the *Hancock* for over a year, once again sailing throughout the Pacific in the capacity of escort and providing support for island invasions.

He sailed the entire Pacific area of the war and participated in almost every major battle in that theater. Scrambling to get to his battle station once, Alex came out of a hatch near a large gun just as it fired, suffering severe hearing loss as a result.

Alex spent over four years at sea. During this time, as he did while in the CCC, he had most of his money sent home to his now widowed mother to help her with her needs. When he got home, she presented him with a savings book for an account containing all the money he had ever sent her. Alex's Pacific war experience finally came full circle, as he had been in the Bay Area when he first learned about the war's start and happened to be there on the day it ended.

Alex Rothe

Lucky

When Harold ("Scat") Scatterday Jr. describes his experiences in WWII, all a person can do is keep shaking his head in amazement and think about how incredibly lucky Scat is to be sitting there telling you his story.

Scat and four other school buddies from Pueblo, Colorado, headed off to the Army together, and after basic training they went out to the West Coast to prepare to go overseas. Scat's dad drove out to see them before they shipped out. He took them out to dinner and asked Scat's friend Louie Hard, "So, Louie, what are you going to do after the war, go to work for your dad?" Without a second of hesitation, Louie looked him in the eyes and said, "Mr. Scatterday, I won't be coming back." Scat and Louie shipped off together to Saipan as replacements. There they were split up, as Scat went to the 77th Infantry Division and Louie to the 96th. A short time later, Scat wrote Louie a letter, but it came back. Louie had been killed in action. Scat and the three others would all return home.

Now with the 307th Infantry Regiment, Co. G of the 77th, Scat was part of the invasion of Okinawa. This is the point in his story where you really start shaking your head in amazement. As his company was climbing down the cargo nets from the ship to the landing craft, a kamikaze slammed into the other side of the ship, wiping out the entire HQ Company of the 307th. The invasion forces landed in the middle of the island, and in short order the island was cut in half. The Marines started north, and the Army started south, which was where the fiercest fighting would be. The Allies were now on Japanese soil, so the Japanese were dug in, and the fighting, which was almost like the trench warfare during WWI, was more difficult than it had ever been to that point in the war.

Scat was a bazooka man, and he moved around to wherever he was needed. But neither he nor anyone else moved around at night. Nighttime was terrifying, as the Japanese were constantly trying to infiltrate the American lines. Anything that moved was shot. "You just hunkered down in your foxhole and stayed still." Scat remembers that the code word was "wonderful pickle," because the Japanese couldn't pronounce it. Two nighttime experiences stick out in his mind—one eerie and one that still makes him laugh. The first happened as he and his foxhole mate were sitting in the pitch-black darkness, and a flare was sent up to illuminate the area. They looked up and saw the silhouette of a Japanese soldier standing at the rim of their foxhole. He must have been just as startled, for he turned around and ran. The funny experience occurred when Scat and a foxhole mate were looking out of their hole and thought they saw something move. His partner asked whether they should toss out a grenade. Scat said they should not do anything until they knew for sure. As soon as it was determined that the movement hadn't been caused by anything threatening, Scat noticed his foxhole mate searching around on the floor of the foxhole. He had already pulled the pin of the grenade and was now looking for it to put it back in.

Most everything else that happened on Okinawa wasn't funny, however. One time when Scat was sitting on the edge of his foxhole, a shell landed about a foot and half from his hip. Fortunately it was a dud. Another time he and three other soldiers were pinned down with machine gun fire, and he was the only one to survive. Another night they were ordered to make a major push forward. As they all started running across an open expanse, a soldier crossed right in front of Scat and at that instant was hit by a bullet.

Of the 160 men in his company, Scat was one of only sixteen who was able to walk off the island. He had not a scratch on him.

The ship sent to pick up the troops was equipped to take care of 160 men, so the sixteen survivors lived well on the trip back to the Philippines. Once they had returned to the Philippines, Co. G was brought back to full strength with replacements and then began training for the planned invasion of the Japanese homeland, but the atomic bombs were dropped, and the war ended before the invasion happened. Scat and his company went on to Japan anyway as part of the occupation forces. He found it strange that as they drove or marched through the towns, there were no people to be found. The civilians had been told throughout the war that the Americans were monsters who would rape, pillage, and murder everyone. It took a full month before people realized that this wasn't true and started emerging from hiding. Scat found the people to be very friendly and docile. He was sent to the northern island of Hokkaido, where he was put in charge of a Japanese coal mine operation. The 77th was deactivated while he was there, and he was transferred to the 5th Air Force in Tokyo for a short time until he earned enough points to go home. One of the things he remembers about his time in Tokyo was that he slept in sheets for the first time in two years.

After the war, Scat returned home, got a degree in architecture, and went into the lumberyard business with his dad. They built it into a successful company that Scat has since passed on to his children. Scat will tell you that he truly was the luckiest when he met and married his wife, Janice. His good fortune continued with the birth of his two children, his grandson, and his two great-grandchildren.

Harold "Scat" Scatterday, Jr.

Stumbled into Service

Dick Scholl, who was born and raised in Milwaukee, chuckles as he describes how he got into the Army. He had been dating a girl who accepted a job in Panama. She asked him to go with her, but Dick wasn't in any financial shape to do so. He later heard that a couple of guys he knew had enlisted in the Army and were going to Panama, and he thought that would be his ticket to get there. He was working at a bank and enlisted during his lunch break on October 7, 1941, exactly two months before Pearl Harbor.

Dick was sent down to Texas for his basic training. He was on a weekend leave, which would be his only leave over the next four years, and was with a buddy at a movie theater when suddenly across the screen flashed the words: PEARL HARBOR HAS BEEN ATTACKED. ALL MILITARY PERSONNEL REPORT BACK TO BASE IMMEDIATELY.

He was soon moved to New Orleans and then onto a ship sailing—of all places—to Panama. He became part of the 158th Regimental Combat Team (the Bushmasters) and would spend the next eight months guarding the Canal and undergoing jungle training. It was a shock for a boy from the upper Midwest. He also had a chance to meet up with that old girlfriend, who by now had married. From Panama, the 158th boarded a ship for the Pacific.

The 158th landed in Australia to regroup. From there they proceeded to New Guinea and began fighting their way toward Japan. They were involved in a number of beach and island invasions in New Guinea before heading up to take part in the invasion of the Philippines. Conditions were very rough, and you could never let your guard down. He remembers how the Japanese would shimmy up palm trees at night and start picking off soldiers in the morning as they stood in the chow line. Another time, as he covered himself with his poncho at night, something big brushed against him. The next morning he and his foxhole mate concluded that it was a large snake. During the three years he was in the Pacific, Dick spent 330 days in combat.

One day, after some fighting in the Philippines, Dick was resting against a palm tree when his commander came up to him and told him to gather his things. His enlistment was up, and he was now going home. It was a relief, as the 158th had been selected to spearhead the planned invasion of the Japanese homeland. Dick was at sea when the atomic bombs were dropped, ending the war and saving the 158th from what would have been a suicide mission.

Dick remembers arriving in San Francisco at midnight to a lit-up mess hall. "It was so bright. I hadn't seen a light bulb in three years. I also hadn't seen ice cream, donuts, steaks, and other food they had set out for us. It was a wonderful feast," Dick recalls. He also vividly remembers returning home and still gets emotional when he describes what it meant to see his family again. It was so good to be home now, but the war had taken its toll on Dick. He lost all his teeth due to the poor nutrition while overseas, he was hospitalized with a malaria attack on his wedding day, and there were the recurring bad memories. Despite these road bumps, Dick has had a great walk through life, with a wonderful wife and family and a career in banking, which he concluded as a branch president.

Dick Scholl

Cowboy at Sea

Ron Sinclair grew up on the high plains of Wyoming and is a cowboy in the truest sense. Growing up, he did ranching work, such as breaking horses and driving cattle. Prior to going into the service, he drove a herd of forty-seven horses eighty miles from Cheyenne into the mountains of Colorado. When the war broke out, he initially took an agricultural deferment. Later he declined another one and enlisted. When he enlisted, he asked not to be put into the Navy, as he wasn't sure how he would do in the confined spaces of a ship and also because he didn't know how to swim. He was assigned to the Navy.

After boot camp in Idaho, Ron went to the West Coast and joined the crew of the aircraft carrier USS *Marcus Island* as it set sail for the Pacific Theater. Being at sea was very foreign to this cowboy. As he tells it, "We had had a long dry spell in Wyoming, and the only bodies of water I saw were the occasional mud puddle. Now the only thing I could see in every direction was water." He also didn't care for palm trees he saw on the islands. "Pretty trees, but they didn't offer much shade." Although an aircraft carrier is big, it was confining for Ron, after growing up on the wide-open prairie. Ron would be at sea, without returning home, for the next three and a half years.

During those three and a half years, Ron had numerous close calls. The first involved a fire that broke out on the flight deck. Ron used a water hose to try to keep things as cool as possible, aware that the deck right below him was where the fuel and bombs were stored.

Another time he was given the opportunity to go up on one of the planes from the carrier. He was all strapped in, ready to go, when an officer came up. The officer decided he wanted to go on the flight instead, and he kicked Ron out of the plane. When the plane returned later, both it and the officer were badly shot up.

Ron's closest call came during the battle of Mindoro. The *Marcus Island* was attacked by three kamikazes. Ron's battle station was on the gun mount at the bow of the ship. Two of the kamikazes crashed just off the bow of the ship, with one clipping the safety rail right above him. Pieces of shrapnel flew everywhere, and one piece hit Ron in the head, knocking him out. That piece of shrapnel was flat on one side, while the rest of it had sharp, jagged edges. The flat end hit him; otherwise he would have been killed.

As Ron now looks down at that piece of shrapnel, which he kept as a memento, he shakes his head as he thinks of all those close calls and reflects, “All I can figure is that the good Lord was looking out for me during that time.”

Ron Sinclair

Paper Fan and Chopsticks

Right after they graduated from high school in the small town of Alluwe, Oklahoma, Amos ("Bill") Standeford's older brother was drafted by the Army Air Corps. Bill, fourteen months younger, had wanted to go to school with his brother so badly that he entered school early, and he too graduated in 1943. Once again, he wanted to follow his brother and enlist in the Army Air Corps, but he needed his father's signature because he was under eighteen, and his father would not let his two sons serve at the same time. A month later, though, Bill received his notice and was drafted into the Army.

Boot camp was easy for Bill, largely due to his upbringing. "My dad was the toughest man I ever knew," Bill says. "But he was also very fair, honest, and hardworking." Bill developed those same traits, and they served him well during his time in the Army and throughout his life.

After boot camp, his group gathered on the West Coast to board a ship heading for New Caledonia as replacements. Taking advice about the best way to handle the ocean crossing from an uncle who served in WWI, Bill made the sea journey without getting seasick. This certainly wasn't the case for the vast majority of men, most of whom, like Bill, were on a ship for the first time.

Landing in New Caledonia, Bill was assigned to Co. B, 27th Infantry Regiment of the 25th Infantry Division. He quickly rose from being a lowly private to a 1st Scout and eventually a platoon leader. From New Caledonia, the 25th entered the battle to liberate the Philippines. While spearheading his unit as the 1st Scout, Bill suffered shrapnel wounds. After a couple of weeks recovering—he still has a piece of shrapnel in his shoulder—he rejoined his unit. Soon after, while charging the front lines, he was wounded again. Both times, on the day he was wounded, back home in Oklahoma a mother's intuition kicked in, and his mom told his dad that she had this feeling Bill was hurt! The second injury took him out of the fighting for good. Once recovered, he spent time at a POW camp guarding prisoners and was training for the invasion of the Japanese homeland when the war ended.

Along with his medals, Bill possesses two mementos from the war: a paper fan and a set of chopsticks, both taken from a Japanese soldier he killed. He didn't relish the fact that he had to kill, but it came down to being in a position of kill or be killed. Many years later, while at the VA for a medical evaluation, a psychiatrist asked him whether he had killed any Japanese, and he said that he had. She then probed further and asked him how many, and he responded, "I was never in a situation to take the time to stop and count."

Bill's homecoming after the war was something he will always remember. It felt so good being home with his mom, dad, and younger brothers and eating his mom's delicious home-cooked meals. A few weeks later his brother, who flew in a B-17 over Europe, returned home, completing the wonderful reunion. Before they left for the war, Bill's dad had opened a pint of whiskey and poured the three of them a drink. He told them they would finish it when everyone came home. On the night of his brother's return, his dad went to the cupboard and pulled out that untouched bottle.

Amos Standeford

Love of the Silent Service

During World War II, 52 submarines out of a fleet of 288 were sunk. One out of every five submariners, or 3,505 men, were killed in action. Submarine veterans of World War II never consider their fellow submariners "lost." Rather, because they went down with their ship in the service of their country and are now entombed in their final resting place beneath the sea, they and their boats are on "eternal patrol." These were the odds that John Votrobek Jr. faced during his time in the "silent service." He beat even greater odds. John had three good friends at submarine school who all buddied around together, and he would be the only one who came home alive.

Being in the submarines didn't even appear on John's radar when he entered the service. He and a buddy initially tried to join the Marines, but their quota was full, so the two young men went home and waited to get drafted. When that time came, John joined the Navy. After his basic training, he was sent to radio school. One night the Navy showed a movie about submarines and then asked for volunteers. John says that something about the submarines struck a chord with him that night, and he volunteered.

John laughs now telling the stories about how his decision didn't hit a chord with his parents. His father, who works for the railroad, took a train up to John's base upon hearing the news to find out what the hell he was doing. His mother, who stayed home crying the day the family saw John off to the service, asked years later, when John's brother joined the paratroopers during the Korean War, "What did I do to deserve this? One son jumps out of planes, and the other went under the sea."

Volunteering for the submarines is one thing, but actually getting into it is another. It is a very difficult program to be accepted into. Candidates go through a stringent battery of physical, psychological, and water/diving tests. John passed the initial physical and was sent to submarine school in New London, Connecticut, where he went through this battery of tests. In addition to passing all these tests to demonstrate that you have the makeup to be in the submarines, you have to know everything about the submarine itself. Although John's main job would be as the radioman, to graduate from the school you had to know every position on the sub in case you were called to replace a crew member who was unable to fulfill his duties. John excelled, and he graduated, getting his dolphin pin.

From sub school, John took a journey halfway around the world. From the States he headed to New Guinea and from there to Brisbane, Australia, down to Sydney and Melbourne, and then clear across the country to the west coast city of Perth, where the submarine base was located. The wonderful treatment of the submariners by the Aussies led them to incorporate the Aussie bush hat into their uniform. John did initial work at the base, tending subs there between missions. He was then assigned to the USS *Blenny*. The *Blenny* had already been on one patrol, and John would go on its next three.

His first mission was the wildest of the three. Off the coast of Vietnam the *Blenny* endured eight hours of depth charges. During this time they had to shut things down to maintain silence, and the temperature in the sub reached 135 degrees. Later in the patrol, the top hatch was not fully secured during one dive. John and the skipper were in the conning tower and quickly had to seal off their hatch from the main compartments. The water in the conning tower was up to their waists before the sub was able to resurface.

His second patrol was largely considered "lifeguard duty," which meant being on call to rescue downed pilots in the sea. His third and the last patrol on the *Blenny* involved boarding Chinese junkets, which the Japanese were now using, looking for contraband. Another submarine on the same duty, the USS *Cod*, came under attack during such a search, and five crew members were stranded on the junket. Three days later, the *Blenny* came up to inspect a junket and discovered the five crew men, rescued them, and returned them to their sub. John got to know two of those men, and they were lifelong friends until the other men's deaths.

The *Blenny* patrolled in the southwest Pacific, making runs between Perth and the Philippines. Altogether it sank nine big ships and sixty-four small ships—a record. Patrols normally lasted between forty and sixty days. Between patrols, crews were sent to a rest and relaxation camp for two weeks to get away from their duties and from the war. During this time their sub was refitted.

When asked what life and conditions were like on a submarine during those long periods at sea, John says they were actually pretty good. The food was the best in the Navy. The sub was air- conditioned and comfortable in that regard, unless they came under attack and had to shut everything down. During these times, the air could get so bad you couldn't get a match to light. The men took bucket baths, using the fresh water collected from the air conditioner condensers. The sub was three hundred feet long and twenty feet wide (with fourteen feet of actual interior space). It was somewhat cramped, but as John looks back on it, he never felt claustrophobic. He does add, though, that he would never be able to handle life on the sub now.

The men of the *Blenny* and submariners in general have remained a very close-knit group through the years. They have a strong association and had many reunions and gatherings until recently, when time had diminished their numbers. In 1989 John and other crew members gathered off the coast of Maryland to see the *Blenny* go off on an eternal patrol of its own when it was sunk to make an artificial reef.

John Votrobeck, Jr.

Lied to the President

Henry ("Gil") Wilson's fascinating story is almost something out of a Hollywood movie. And in fact Hollywood plays a part in his story.

Gil's war experience centered around his interest in photography. He went to a Los Angeles area vocational high school that taught photography and freelanced as a photographer for several LA newspapers. After high school he worked for Eastman Kodak in Hollywood.

Gil enlisted in the Army Air Corps shortly after Pearl Harbor. His photography background didn't seem to matter to the Army, and he was sent off to become an aircraft mechanic. Walking to his first class, he happened to see a sign saying PHOTO SECTION on a building and decided to investigate. He told the officer in charge about his photography experience, and the next day he was transferred to the photography unit.

Gil photographed base activities, and one assignment was to photograph a visiting general from Washington. The photographer accompanying the general happened to be a classmate from his high school, and he told Gil of a new film unit being formed in Hollywood. Gil put in for a transfer and was moved to the First Motion Picture Unit. The FMPU made training films for the military.

After some time in his new assignment, Gil heard rumors that a unit was being sent to China to document the war. Gil was excited about the idea and went to see the adjutant in charge about being selected. The adjutant was a Capt. Ronald Reagan. He told Gil to go home for the weekend and talk it over with his parents, and if they agreed, he would consider it. Gil already had two brothers overseas, so he wasn't about to say anything to his parents. He returned on Monday and told Reagan that his parents were supportive. "I bold-faced lied to the future president of the United States," Gil says with a chuckle.

Gil was soon with the 16th Combat Camera Unit heading for China. The trip there was an adventure in itself. They took a ship to Australia and then on to India. Then they took a train east across India and boarded a plane that flew them over the Himalayas. Once in China, they were attached to the 14th Air Force, the Flying Tigers.

Gil flew twenty-five missions with the 14th, as well as going on ground missions with the Chinese Army. On his twenty-fifth mission, the day the first atomic bomb was dropped, his plane was hit, and they were forced to bail out. It was nighttime, and soon after Gil pulled the cord of his parachute, he hit the ground hard. He had hit the side of a mountain! The impact injured his leg and knocked him out. He eventually came to, and when daylight arrived, he started walking. He soon heard a faint cry for help and found a badly hurt crew member. Gil got him comfortable and then left to go find help.

Gil came across a Chinese farmer who told him of a busy road farther on. The road turned out to be the Burma Road. An Army truck eventually came along, and Gil flagged them down. He explained the situation, but the two soldiers weren't really listening. Instead, they kept talking about a big bomb that had been dropped and how the war would soon be over. Another jeep finally came along. It went for help, and soon a strange contraption came flying in. It was the first helicopter Gil had ever seen. Gil's and his injured friend's ordeals were soon over. For his efforts, Gil received the Air Medal, the Bronze Star, and the Purple Heart.

Gil went on to have a fascinating life that continues to this day. After the war he became a photographer for Hollywood magazines. He would meet and befriend many celebrities while in the industry. He then became a detective with the Los Angeles Police Department, and ultimately owned numerous successful businesses. Fortunately his life is recorded in the thousands upon thousands of photographs he has taken. He's presently busy cataloging all these photographs for his family.

Gil Wilson

European Theater
(ETO)

Disrupted Life

The bombing of Pearl Harbor greatly disrupted Lee Anderson's world. Lee was a freshman in college when he heard the news. His parents, both natives of their community in western Minnesota, decided to move to Portland, Oregon, where the economy was booming, thanks to the war industry there. Lee helped them move out in 1942 and spent that summer working there. He was astounded that he was getting paid an unheard-of $60 a week. He returned to the University of Minnesota in the fall and toward the end of the semester enlisted under the Army's delayed entry program, which would allow him to finish college. Despite having entered the program, he was drafted midway through the following spring semester.

Now in the Army, Lee entered a very long period of uncertainty during which he was given little, if any, information about his situation. After training, he boarded a troop ship that crossed the Atlantic, through the Straits of Gibraltar, and landed in Algeria. There he spent a couple of weeks in a repo depot before boarding a train that he rode for five days across the Sahara Desert while sitting on the floor of a forty by eight (forty men or eight horses) boxcar. Each GI was issued a duffel bag and, for some reason, a mattress cover. When they made stops at stations, the GIs would trade with the locals, and one of the items they traded was that Army-issued duffel bag. Lee laughs as he tells of looking out across the train platforms and seeing locals wearing these duffel bags as pants, with two holes cut out for their legs and some GI's name and serial number stenciled on their butts.

Finally, after all the time he had served and the long distances he had traveled, he got an answer about his situation. He was being assigned to the 45th Infantry Division, ending up in Co. F, 2nd Battalion, 179th Infantry Regiment.

He met up with the 45th in Salerno, crossed over to Italy, and began the move up the spine of the country. He remembers this as a miserable time. It was a very wet fall, and the troops were out in the elements in their foxholes. They remained wet the entire time. On December 5, Lee incurred the first of his two battle wounds. During a heavy artillery barrage, he was hit with shrapnel in the upper left arm. When asked what it is like to go through an artillery barrage, he tells you it is frightening. He also says that the most haunting sound during these barrages was hearing the cries of "Medic, Medic!" off in the distance.

Lee was evacuated to a hospital in Naples. While lying in his hospital bed recovering, he was going through his personal possessions and came across his prayer book, which had been in his chest pocket. Lodged in it was a chunk of shrapnel. The book saved his life. Although he was seriously injured, Lee's time in the hospital was pleasant, since he was out of the elements and sleeping in a bed. After recovering, he rejoined his unit prior to their amphibious landing at Anzio.

The invasion at Anzio initially seemed easy, as the Allies quickly landed and established a beachhead with little resistance. Things grew worse as they started moving inland, however, for the Germans were entrenched in the surrounding hills. As Lee's unit moved forward, they got too far ahead of their comrades and were surrounded. At one point they were so close to the enemy that German tanks rolled over their foxholes, crushing the stock of one of his foxhole mates' rifle. They eventually made it back to their lines. Soon thereafter, though, Lee was wounded for the second time, getting hit in the back of the head with shrapnel. He found himself back in the same hospital he had just left weeks earlier.

Lee recovered just in time to rejoin his unit prior to the invasion of southern France. It was a relatively easy landing, and the Allies started racing north, with the Germans in full retreat. Once again, Lee's unit got too far ahead and were surrounded and captured by the Germans. The Germans knew at this point, however, that their situation was hopeless. Lee and his fellow captives knew it too and over time managed to talk the Germans into surrendering to them!

Returning to the Allied lines with the roles now reversed, they came under attack by members of the Free French Underground, who mistook them for Germans. After they convinced their captors that they were Americans, they were met with hugs and kisses by the Frenchmen. It was a little more difficult to convince the French to let them keep their German prisoners, who wouldn't have fared so well if the French had taken them into custody.

The Allies were continuing their push north through France when Lee succumbed to a bad case of trench foot. This was what finally took Lee off the front lines for good. He was deemed no longer combat able and was transferred to Supreme Headquarters. The worst of the war was finally over for Lee.

Lee's new role at the Supreme Headquarters of the American Expeditionary Forces (SHAEF) was to secure accommodations for the American headquarters. The Allies were quickly starting to push the Germans back into Germany, and as the front lines moved, so did their headquarters. Lee and his party moved in advance of the rest of the headquarters and found a place—usually a castle or hotel—that would accommodate the staff and got it prepped or renovated for their staff's arrival. He remembers arriving in Frankfurt and finding the city so pulverized by the Allied bombings and fighting as the battle line passed through the city that he had to go up in a Piper airplane to try to find a good location. In his position at SHAEF, he interacted with the likes of Generals Eisenhower, Bradley, and Patton.

Lee left Europe with a Bronze Star and two Purple Hearts. He returned to Minnesota to resume the life that the war had interrupted. He finished his college degree, went on to get advanced degrees, and had a long and distinguished career in higher education. For the last twenty-eight years of his career he served as a dean of libraries at Colorado State University.

Lee Anderson

Christmas Eve Dinner

Nolan Ashburn is the son of the first American wounded in World War I. His dad never recovered from his wounds and died when Nolan was three and a half years old. Years later, Nolan was a freshman in college when Pearl Harbor was bombed. The attack took place on a Sunday, and his mother wasn't able to reach him until Monday night. She told him to remember what happened to his father and admonished him to stay in school and not join up. She was too late. Nolan and all the members of his boarding house had enlisted first thing Monday morning.

Nolan did stay in college while going through ROTC. He was finally shipped out to basic training after his sophomore year. After training he was selected for the Army Specialized Training Program (ASTP) and went off for what amounted to another year of college. After D-Day, however, the army projected a shortage of combat troops, and the ASTP program was canceled. Nolan was subsequently sent to join the 424th Infantry Regiment of the newly formed 106th Infantry Division.

The division shipped out to England and spent a short period training there. Spirits were high, as the war was going well for the Allies. The news was so good that everyone assumed they would go over to the Continent as part of the occupation forces. They crossed the Channel into France and continued on to Belgium, where they relieved the 2nd Infantry Division. Everything continued to look good, as the 2nd hadn't seen any action on this section of the front lines in six weeks. Word spread through the ranks that the war would be over by Christmas.

On December 16, 1944, after the 106th had been on the line for only four days, the Germans started the massive attack that came to be known as the Battle of the Bulge. The 106th was spread thin, over a twenty-seven-mile line, and none of the troops had any combat experience. Nolan himself, short of his basic training, had spent his entire time in the Army in school and had even less knowledge of combat tactics. The Germans quickly overran the area, surrounding Nolan's regiment and forcing two other regiments to surrender. Everything was chaotic. "We hadn't been there long enough to get our bearings, so you didn't know which way was which or which way to run," Nolan recalls.

During the next ten days, Nolan roamed through the forest with no food or sleep, inadequately dressed for what was the coldest winter in Europe in fifty years. Nolan's feet were frozen, and he remembers hoping he could feel his feet one last time before he died. When asked how he thinks he managed to survive that situation, he answers, "You turn into an animal just trying to survive." The highlight of this time was his Christmas Eve dinner. Someone had found a frozen can of corned beef hash alongside the road, and Nolan and three other soldiers used their bayonets to open the can and chip away at the contents. The overcast skies finally cleared on December 26, and planes began dropping in supplies. The Allies started driving the Germans back to Germany, which was the beginning of the end of the war.

When the war ended, Nolan spent time guarding prisoners and was at Camp Lucky Strike in France, awaiting a ship to take the 106th to fight in the Pacific Theater, when Japan surrendered. The camp erupted in celebration upon hearing the news.

After what Nolan's mother had heard from his father about his experiences in World War I, she told Nolan when he returned home that she could not bear to hear about his experiences. She had suffered with worry about her only child while he was in harm's way and now only wanted to enjoy the relief and happiness of his being home.

Nolan Ashburn

Dumb Luck

Ray Babcock says that if he ever wrote a book about his life, he would entitle it *Dumb Luck.* He says he has been in situations too numerous to count where he can only write off his survival as dumb luck.

Ray grew up in the woods of Vermont and was drafted—and enlisted—to serve during World War II. He was first drafted, and, after going through all the paperwork and testing, he was told that he should to go into the Cadet Training Program. He agreed to do this, although he had never even touched an airplane. There was a snag, though. His serial number started with a three, which meant he had been drafted and was thus ineligible for the program. Because his test scores were so high, they came up with a way to get around this problem. He was discharged and told to come back and enlist in the Army Air Corps. He was now off to Specialized Basic Training. Just as he started the program, however, all the cadets were told that there was an abundance of pilots, and the program was being discontinued. The students now had their choice of either infantry or gunnery. The "choice" was made by a red line drawn across the middle of each page where the students were listed. Those above the red line on the page went to gunnery, while the bottom half went to infantry. Ray's name was on the upper half on the second page.

Gunnery school took Ray all over the country, primarily in the Southwest. Arizona was starkly different from the lush woods of Vermont. While there, he took an interesting tour of the Grand Canyon. Standing out at the flight line one day, he was waved over to a two-seat plane. A plane had crashed in the Canyon, and they were going to drop supplies to the survivors. Ray was put in the backseat with supplies piled on top of him. They flew down into the Canyon, and the pilot told him when to drop the supplies out of the plane. Later, while out with his B-17 crew on a training mission, Ray told the story over the plane's intercom. The pilot was taken by the story, and soon the lumbering bomber was flying in the Canyon. Looking out the waist gunner's window, Ray was looking up at the rim.

Its training complete, the crew headed to pick up its own B-17 and prepare to go to Europe. The crew members were told that no more B-17s were needed in Italy, so they took a train to Virginia and boarded a ship to go to Europe as a replacement crew. They arrived in Italy at Foggia Air Base. They were housed in tents in an area Ray describes as one big mud hole. They were given tents that they had to set up themselves, and since it was winter, they had to improvise a heat source. Ray built a stove out of truck parts that burned aviation fuel. One night he woke up feeling hot and found the tent engulfed in flames. He escaped wearing only shorts and one sock.

Ray and his crew were scheduled for missions almost immediately, but just prior to his first one, he experienced something that really shook him. He was out on the flight line when he and an officer next to him watched as a plane shot off flares, signifying that it had injured men on board. It was the officer's plane, and he asked Ray to help him when the plane came to a stop. When they opened the door, what they saw inside was horrifying. The fuselage was completely covered with human remains. The two waist gunners had been killed by an exploding artillery shell. The officer collapsed from shock and grief and was taken away on a gurney.

Ray and his crew were on their sixth mission with the 773rd Bomb Squad of the 463rd Bomb Group when their plane was hit over Vienna. The plane went into a nosedive, and the next thing Ray knew, everything was silent and gray. He wondered where he was until he looked "up" to see the ground fast approaching. He pulled the rip cord of his parachute and immediately flipped upright, the force of this maneuver blowing off his boots. He remembers the bizarre sight of his fur-lined boots, sitting neatly side by side, floating off into the sky. When he landed, he was captured by locals and turned over to the military. He was now a POW.

The trip to the POW camp was fraught with danger. Along the way, the train was strafed by a couple of P-47s, and as the POWs marched to a different train station in Munich, the locals threw stones and bricks at them. Once they reached the station, it came under attack by bombers, and they were forced to lie out in the open. Ray was thrown up and down on the ground by the percussion of the bombs and was black-and-blue when the attack was over. On this train trip, he learned that only he and three other crew members (out of nine) from his plane had survived.

The train finally pulled into Stalag 7A, which would be his home for the next couple of months until they were liberated. There wasn't much to do at the camp except wait for the two "meals" of the day. The first was morning tea, which was slightly warm water with what looked like grass clippings in it. The men usually didn't drink it but instead shaved with it because the water was warm. The second meal, consisting mostly of a small piece of bread, some turnip, and maybe a piece of fat in warm water, wasn't much better, as quality and quantity were very poor. After eating their bread, for example, the men spent time picking splinters out of their gums, as the bread was composed mostly of sawdust. Care packages from the Red Cross helped them survive.

One night flares were dropped to mark the camp, and the surrounding area was bombed. A few days later an American tank stuck its turret through the fence. The prisoners were soon ferried in C-47s back to camps in France. In the French camp, Ray was put in a tent full of privates who harassed him. A few days later a plane full of top brass landed. As they walked by, one of the officers stopped and looked at Ray, who was dressed in an Australian hat, tattered flight suit, and German shoes, and asked him what service he was in. The officer then ordered him to take his hat off. When Ray told him that he didn't have another hat, General Eisenhower said, "Better none than that one." Feeling unappreciated by his tent mates and by Ike, Ray left the camp and wandered the French countryside for a month, staying with—and helping—farmers along the way. Finally returning to the States, he hitchhiked home. During this whole period of time, his parents had only received one telegram from the Army, stating that he was missing in action. When he walked up to the house, his dad was under a car that he was working on. He rolled out from under it, looked up at Ray, and said, "'Bout time you came home."

Ray worked a bit after the war but eventually reenlisted in the Air Force and made it a career. When the Korean War broke out, he flew thirty-four missions as a gunner on a B-29. During the Vietnam War, he was told they could use people with his skills in Vietnam. He went home that night and looked at his records. Noticing that he had put in twenty years and three days of service, he resigned the next day, wanting nothing to do with another war. Perhaps he also didn't want to test that dumb luck again in a third war?

Ray Babcock

Leadership

Barney Barnd exemplifies the generation that fought in World War II. He struggled through the Depression, surviving it and going off to do his part to help save the world from evil before returning home and, without missing a beat, doing his part to help make the United States into the economic power it is today.

Barney comes from a hearty, hardworking family. He is proud that he always had a job—from age twelve until the day he retired. His dad told him something once that always stuck with him: "Get up in the morning and do your job, and go to bed at night leaving things a little better than you found them." He vowed always to be successful at whatever he did. From an early age Barney was also a student of business and people, learning everything he could from his experiences. This laid down a solid foundation that prepared him for going off to war and for what followed in the rest of his life.

Barney was drafted in the fall of 1942. Right away something happened that would occur over and over again throughout his military and business careers: he was singled out and called on to do things. He volunteered once when they were looking for a typist, despite having been told that the unwritten rule in the Army is never to volunteer for anything. That rule rubbed Barney the wrong way, since he just isn't that type of guy. He went down to Texas for basic and artillery training and was singled out to be sent to Officer Candidate School. He then married Dottie, and they made a vow that they would stay together while he was still in the States, so they moved together to California when he was transferred there. From California Barney's unit, Battery A of the 569th Coastal Artillery Anti-Aircraft Automatic Weapons Battalion, shipped to North Carolina for maneuvers. When Barney finally got orders to ship overseas, Dottie traveled to New York to see him off.

Barney remembers that when they were leaving New York harbor, he looked at the Statue of Liberty as they sailed past it and said, "Old girl, I hope I see you again." The battalion sailed to England and then crossed the Channel to Le Havre, France, in the fall of 1944. Moving up to the front, Barney's artillery unit was attached to the 278th Field Artillery. The 278th had the largest Allied guns in the European Theater of Operations (ETO), and Barney was responsible for protecting them. They followed the guns everywhere and traveled across Europe with them until the war's end. Being in proximity of those massive guns left Barney with some hearing loss.

Once the front lines had reached Germany, Barney got a call from HQ. Marlene Dietrich, the famous German actress who fled Germany when the Nazis came to power, wanted to pose in front of an American artillery piece on German territory. HQ told Barney to prepare for her visit. The scheduled time came and went without the actress showing up, and it was time to move on. Barney held back an artillery piece and sent on the rest. Dietrich and her entourage arrived two hours late. Barney told the colonel accompanying her that he had had to send the rest of the unit on ahead. Dietrich then said that if this wasn't the real thing, she didn't want any part of it. Barney recounts that he acted like an officer and a gentleman, but inside he was thinking, "Get out of my sight!"

Barney tells stories of compassion that he feels set the US Army apart from previous conquering armies throughout history. One time, they stopped in a village that they thought was completely deserted. The battalion priest, one of a number of people in the Army for whom Barney had deep respect, found a German who told him that everyone was in hiding. He also told the priest that everyone was sad that their church had been badly damaged. Barney and the priest rallied some soldiers, and they cleaned up the church. They rang the bell, and people started appearing. The priest then gave a mass in German.

Farther down the road, Barney was notified that there was an isolated hospital that was in bad shape. The colonel wanted Barney to take some men with a couple of trucks and go investigate it. Along the way, they were stopped by the mayor of a village they were passing through. The mayor told them that he had fifty German soldiers in the village jail cell and their weapons in another cell. He wanted to surrender them and the village to Barney. Barney radioed HQ with the news and waited for orders about what to do. HQ messaged back to tell the mayor to leave the weapons in the cell and to have the men take off any clothing that identified them as soldiers and send them home. Barney found comfort in that message both in the compassion it showed, as well as the sense it gave him that the war was nearing an end.

Arriving at the hospital, Barney was horrified at what he saw. The facility was occupied by severely injured patients from both sides. They had been abandoned by the German army and were out of supplies. He had seen a lot of horrifying things following the front lines across Europe, but this was the saddest thing he experienced. He took a German officer who had stayed behind back to the supply center to get all the medical supplies he needed for his people, and then ambulances came and retrieved the Allied patients.

The 569th made it to the Austrian border, when Barney was chosen to go to Paris for schooling and training in preparation for the postwar occupation of Germany. He was in Paris when VE Day was announced. The city exploded with celebration. The celebration was short-lived for Barney and his men, however, as he returned to his unit a few days later and was told to prepare to depart for the Pacific Theater. They moved to Le Havre and were assigned to help guard the docks while they waited for their transfer. One night about eleven o'clock, Barney was lying in his cot when all of a sudden the warships out in the harbor started shooting their guns and blowing their whistles. The war in the Pacific had come to end. Barney says he put his face in his pillow and cried.

Because an officer needs twice the points that an enlisted man does to qualify to go home, he saw all his men off and performed another year of occupation duties before he made it home to Dottie. When he finally returned home, there were no jobs to be found because so many had gotten home before him during that year. This was where that solid foundation laid down during his childhood came in handy, though it was now even stronger with the leadership and people skills he had learned in the Army.

Barney had saved most of his Army paychecks, and Dottie had saved her paychecks as well. They looked for a business to buy and soon found a car dealership. Eventually they also bought a small manufacturing company. They worked hard and poured everything back into it. They built up the manufacturing company to the point that it was a very attractive investment, and they were bought out. Barney stayed on with the company with which they merged, helping build it into a Fortune 500 company and retiring forty years later as vice president/president of overseas operations. When he is complimented on his success, he says he attributes it to a combination of his upbringing and what he learned in the Army.

Barney Barnd

Fighting in Both Theaters

Very few people can say they were involved in two of the most important events in World War II. And very few people can say that they were shot at by both the Germans and the Japanese during the war. Gordon ("Dick") Breiner is one of the few people who can make both claims!

Dick grew up in Pittsburg, Kansas. After graduating from high school in 1941, he took jobs that really had no future, so he signed up to go to a welding school in California. On December 7 he was visiting his grandparents to say good-bye when they heard the news about Pearl Harbor. His mother asked him not to go to California because she was worried, as were many, that the Japanese were going to invade the West Coast.

Dick did go to California and completed his training, getting certified as a welder. With the buildup for the war now in full force, he easily found work at the shipyards. He helped build Liberty ships. At this point, his shipyard was completing a ship every twenty-nine days. He worked there for a year, and when it became apparent that he was going to be drafted, he quit his job to make one last trip home to Kansas before going into the service.

He was given his choice of services when he returned to California. He chose the Navy, with the idea of getting into the Seabees, where he could use his welding skills. He shipped across the country to the East Coast for training, eventually joining the 81st Construction Battalion, and soon departed for England. This was the stopping-off point before his involvement in the first important event, D-Day.

Dick was aboard an LST (Landing Ship Tank) that landed on Utah Beach at 10:00 a.m. on D-Day. His unit's job was to unload an antiaircraft artillery unit on the ship, and they came under German shelling while doing so. After getting everything unloaded, they tried to leave, but the ship's propellers were broken in the process, forcing them to go back, dig foxholes on the beach, and hunker down. They would end up staying in Normandy through the fall.

They stayed through December, helping rebuild the artificial harbor after a storm destroyed it, as well as unloading ships. Eventually Paris was liberated, giving Dick a chance to see the city. The day they left to return to the States, his sister's husband heard he was there and attempted to visit him. They just missed seeing each other, and by the time Dick made it back to the States, he got word that his brother-in-law had been killed in action.

After a thirty-day leave, his unit regrouped and headed to the Pacific. They traveled through the Panama Canal and made stops in Hawaii and the Marshall Islands before landing on day three of the invasion of Okinawa. While they were there, they came under Japanese shelling and witnessed kamikaze attacks. After finishing their assignment, they headed for Guam to begin training for the planned invasion of the Japanese homeland. The day they arrived in Guam, the Japanese surrendered.

Dick is a good example of someone who is quiet and unassuming and very enjoyable to visit with. Unless you probe further with him, you would never know that he is a walking piece of history, eyewitness to—and part of—some major events in our country's history.

Dick Breiner

Some Closure

Loren Bruns's first experience in World War II involved being detained as a suspected spy. The story isn't something that would be great fodder for the next James Bond novel, though. Instead it is a humorous one. Loren and his buddies, all Kansas farm boys as wet behind the ears as you can get, went out to California on a road trip and mistakenly found themselves in a restricted military area. To make matters worse, they were all of German ancestry with names like Otto and Rudy. The matter was soon cleared up, and they were told they had better get in their car and drive back to Kansas as fast as they could.

Back home in Kansas, Loren had to forego a potentially promising career as a professional baseball player when he was drafted into the Army. He served with the 528th Quartermasters, which were attached to the 45th Division. After Stateside training, he and the 528th set sail across the Atlantic for Africa. In Africa they had additional training and prepared for the planned invasion of Sicily. This invasion would be the first time Allied forces set foot on Axis soil.

The 528th stormed the beaches of Sicily and began the fight to push the Germans off the island. Many memories stick out in Loren's mind from the taking of Sicily: being one of twenty guys responsible for getting 1,700 German and Italian prisoners of war back to the ships; watching waves of planes carrying 82nd Airborne paratroopers being shot out of the sky in a sad case of friendly fire due to mistaken identity; the intense fighting and the numerous close calls he had; and being given an airplane ride by General Patton's personal pilot. The one memory that is seared most darkly into his mind, however, is of watching an American fighter plane crash-land into a pile of artillery shells near his camp. Without concern for his own safety, he ran to the plane to see if he could help out. The pilot was inside the cockpit, slumped over. Everyone was yelling at Loren to get away from the plane, as it was going to blow up. He tried to unstrap the pilot to get him out but couldn't. "I remember looking at his dog tags, which had burnt into his skin—'Lt. Goldenberg, Buffalo, New York'—and then I blanked out from shock, I suppose," Loren recalls, unable to remember what happened next.

A severe medical condition eventually took him out of the war. After initial treatment for blood clots at a hospital in Naples, he was medically evacuated back to the States on the transport ship *Henry Gibbons*. Also aboard with him and about a hundred injured soldiers were a thousand Jewish refugees. This secret refugee evacuation had been undertaken on direct orders from President Roosevelt and handled by Ruth Gruber, a Jewish-American writer and government official. On each side of his ship were other ships full of German POWs in order to discourage German U-boat attacks. This seems to have been effective, since the ship was hunted by German seaplanes and submarines the entire way back to the United States without being sunk.

Loren would spend many months in the hospital recovering. He eventually moved to Colorado, where he operated a successful dairy farm. Through the years, the memory of Lt. Goldenberg was continuously on his mind. He was never able to find out whatever became of the pilot, and that always bothered him. In 2009, soliciting help from a Buffalo newspaper, I found out that Lt. Goldenberg had indeed died that day in the crash. This news finally brought some long overdue closure for Loren.

Loren Bruns

Guardian Angel

If someone ever wanted to get a firsthand account of some of the major battles in the European Theater during World War II, Bill Cameron is a good person to talk to. He participated in most of them. You could also say he had a bird's eye view of many of them, as he served with the famous 82nd Airborne.

One of Bill's brothers was at Pearl Harbor when it was bombed, and two months later, Bill enlisted in the Air Corps to become a pilot. Failing the eye exam, Bill transferred to the Army, where he went to Officers Candidate School and was commissioned as a 2nd lieutenant. Once out of OCS, he and a buddy decided to try to get into the Airborne. After passing the vigorous tests to get into this elite program, Bill shipped off to England in May with the 456th Parachute Field Artillery Battalion of the 82nd Airborne.

On the night of June 5, the 82nd took off from England and parachuted into Normandy ahead of the invasion the next morning. Their objective was to take the town of Sainte Mère-Église. They hoped to draw enemy soldiers from the beaches and also to keep the Germans from sending more support to the beaches. Their assignment was a success, and they eventually linked up with the full invasion force.

They returned to England, regrouped, and prepared for their next assignment, which was to participate in the airborne invasion, called Operation Market Garden, to drive the Germans out of Holland. Thirty-four thousand men were dropped in, making it the largest airborne invasion to date.

Having pushed the Germans back to their border, the 82nd set up camp in France. In December the Battle of the Bulge began, and the 82nd raced to Belgium. Bill was a forward observer at the northern tip of the Bulge when Allied forces pulled back, stranding him and a couple of his men. They were soon taken prisoner by the Germans.

While being marched back to enemy headquarters by the Germans, Bill devised an escape plan. He and the other men distracted their captors and made a run for the forest, eventually reaching the Allied lines. Bill continued to follow the front lines to within fifty miles of Berlin just before the war ended, liberating a concentration camp along the way.

Bill's wife, whom he had married just before deploying, has always said that he has a guardian angel looking over him. She cites as evidence the fact that once, while serving as an aerial observer, he walked away from a plane crash, and another time he just happened to be away from his foxhole when it was shredded by artillery shells.

The 82nd was part of the forces that occupied Berlin after the war, and Bill was stationed there until he accumulated enough points to come home. Returning to his wife and son, who was born while he was overseas, Bill settled back into civilian life until he was called up when the Korean War broke out. Bill again found himself on the front lines, running a radar installation. He would end up staying in the Army and making it his career. After retiring from the Army, he had another long career with the Red Cross. This career had him doing tours in Vietnam, his third war. His wife must have been right about that guardian angel, as Bill made it through three wars unscathed.

Bill Cameron

Living in a Volcano

When you ask Jim Clawson about his World War II experiences, he'll tell you, like many of his fellow veterans, who also say the same thing, that he doesn't have much of a story and that he really didn't do anything. If you probe a little further, however, you'll find that this is not true.

Jim was born and raised in Muncie, Indiana. It was an idyllic life, and he had a great childhood. On December 7, 1941, he was in a friend's basement with his buddies, spinning records and dancing. Suddenly someone interrupted to tell them to turn off the music and listen to reports on the radio about an attack on Pearl Harbor. As it was for much of the nation, the group's first question was, "Where's Pearl Harbor?" That was followed by a second question, particularly relevant for the boys in the group: "What does this mean for us?" That second question was answered for Jim in March of 1943, when he was eighteen and a freshman in college and was drafted into the Army.

After basic training, Jim was sent to Omaha, Nebraska, for signalman's school. Upon graduation, the class prepared to ship overseas. It was discovered during a physical that Jim had a hernia, and he was held back to have an operation. After his surgery, Jim continued overseas. His troop ship first landed in Scotland. He was then put on another ship, destination unknown. A couple of days out to sea, some of the men asked a sailor where they were heading. He just laughed and answered, "Iceland."

In Iceland Jim became a radioman at a radar installation that was part of the Signal Aircraft Warning Group. The purpose of this group was to scan the skies for enemy aircraft. This is where Jim's contention that he didn't do anything in the war falls apart. The shipping channels of the north Atlantic were a vital route in the war effort and keeping them safe so that supplies, equipment, and personnel could get to Europe was crucial.

Jim was stationed at Camp Vail, which was located inside the rim of a dormant volcano. The camp was remote and isolated, and only thirty men were stationed there. There was very little to do at the camp when they were not on duty, and only seldom did they get a chance to get away to Reykjavik, the capital. The weather was dismal most of the year, and they had to deal with the darkness in the winter and the endless sunlight in the summer. While there was plenty to eat, the choice of food usually came down to Spam, Spam, or Spam. Jim does have one fond memory of his fifteen months in Iceland. "The aurora borealis is absolutely incredible. We used to make recliners in the snow and watch it. Far better than any fireworks show I have seen since," he fondly recalls.

The war finally ended, and Jim returned home. He finished college and went on to a thirty-year career in banking. He also met Anne, who became his wife. They have been married for sixty years and have three children and five grandchildren.

It is said that for every soldier on the front lines during WWII, between seven and nine others were needed in support. Winning the war was a massive collective effort, both on the part of everyone in the military and those on the home front. Jim may try to tell you he didn't do anything special. Sorry, Jim, I respectfully disagree. You did your part!

Jim Clawson

Life as an Infantryman

The first thing William Dohrn did after graduating from high school was to enlist in the service, figuring that if he enlisted, he could choose the Navy. It didn't work out the way he wanted it to, though. After signing the enlistment papers, he went to the induction ceremony, where he got in the line for the Navy. When he finally worked his way up to the front, they told him that their quota for the day was filled and that he needed to go stand in the other line. So he was inducted into the Army.

Things continued to go awry for Bill. He planned on getting into the artillery, but after winning an expert marksmanship badge, he was put into the infantry. He would go on to serve with the 60th Infantry Regiment of the 9th Infantry Division. After training in Texas, he shipped off to Europe. After some time in England, he crossed the Channel to France and went on to Belgium and the front lines.

It was February of 1945. The Battle of the Bulge was over, and the Allies were now in the middle of the final push into Germany. Bill was coming up as a replacement soldier. Along the way, he saw firsthand the horrors of war: cities and villages completely leveled; dead, bloated animals everywhere; hungry and desperate civilians. He also experienced the extreme hardships that infantrymen endure. He chipped away at frozen ground to dig foxholes, ate cold rations from cans, and shaved with ice-cold water. He never got more than a couple hours of sleep. "I learned to sleep standing up or leaning against a tank. It took me a long time afterwards to adjust to sleeping in a bed, as I got so used to the ground," Bill says. "The one thing I never got used to was being out in the elements for weeks on end. I am a farm boy from Minnesota, so I was used to being out in the cold, but [before the war] I always had a hot meal and warm bed to go back to at night."

Bill figured that he probably wouldn't survive the war, and he almost didn't—a number of times. One time that stands out above the rest was when his unit moved into a new position and was told to dig in. Bill and his partner found an old foxhole. They found some straw to put into it and an old door to put over it and were very happy with how comfortable they had made it. Their sergeant then came along and told them he didn't like the position they were in and to move farther up. They moved, dug a new foxhole, and cursed that sergeant all night long as an artillery barrage raged. The next morning when they moved out, they walked by their old foxhole. It had taken a direct hit, and there was nothing left of it.

Near the end of the war, while out on patrol, Bill and another soldier came across one hundred German soldiers who surrendered to them. "I wasn't sure which way it was going to go until we got them back to camp," Bill recalls.

The war finally ended, but Bill stayed in Germany for another year as part of the occupation forces. After what he went through, he hates war and wishes no one would ever have to experience it again. But now in his eighties and weakened by terminal cancer, he says, "I would still grab my shotgun in the closet and go defend this wonderful country if I had to."

Bill Dohrn

Memories

Based on his razor-sharp memory and quick wit, you would never know that Bob Forrest is one hundred years old. Not only can he rattle off dates, locations, people he served with, and situations he was in during World War II, he distinctly remembers when World War I ended. "I was six years old and riding my tricycle around an oak tree in the yard when I heard the news," Bob recalls.

When Bob first enlisted in the Army, it was still much like the army of World War I, which moved around primarily on the backs of horses. By the time he was called up for WWII and sent off to Europe, America had begun to modernize, and he was now riding in a tank. Bob was captain (eventually reaching the rank of major) of Co. D, 15th Tank Battalion, 6th Armored Division of Patton's 3rd Army.

While life as a tanker was somewhat easier than being an infantryman, it was still no cakewalk. It was very cramped inside, but Bob says they got used to it. They lived and slept in their tanks, which kept them out of the elements, but they had to leave the top hatch open whenever possible, since otherwise water dripped off the ceiling because of the humidity. They set their boots on the engine in the morning to thaw them out.

Bob led his company of eighteen tanks as they fought their way across Europe after landing on Utah beach two months after D-Day. In the course of doing so, he was awarded the Silver Star (the third-highest combat military decoration) and the Bronze Star for taking charge on leaderless battlefields and leading two separate and successful attacks. He was wounded twice and thus also has two Purple Hearts. The second injury, which took him out of the fighting, happened when, living up to his philosophy of never ordering his men to do something he wouldn't do himself, he climbed out of his tank with a couple of men to rout some Germans out of their foxholes. While doing so, he was hit by a sniper. The bullet went through his left arm—he was never able to grip properly again—and then through his torso. He had code papers tucked inside his pants, and they prevented the bullet from going through his intestines; it went through his stomach instead. He spent the next four months in the hospital, returning to his men three days after Germany surrendered.

He had a wide spectrum of experiences from the humorous (which he says, chuckling, he isn't sure should be printed) to the bad (which were so horrific that he thinks they couldn't be printed). In between are two memories that still stick with him to this day. The first was a thought he had as he was going into battle: "I remember thinking, I'm trying to kill that German, and that German is trying to kill me, and we don't even know each other!" The second memory is of the rare time when a kitchen truck made it up to the line to give them a hot meal. In one line were soldiers waiting to be served. There was a second line of locals at the trash can, where they waited to get the scraps. "Every time I leave the table after a meal and see uneaten food on someone's plate, I think of those people."

All in all, he has never let the bad memories get to him. "I just realized that unfortunately that was how the war was," he says with a shrug.

Bob Forrest

Recurring Thoughts

Years after the war when he was a popular music teacher, Bill Funke would often have thoughts about his war experience while leading the school choir or directing the band. He says they weren't bad flashbacks, but rather thoughts about why this or that friend had to die, the locations and situations he was in, etc.

Bill served in Co. A of the 17th Armored Infantry Battalion of the 12th Armored Division. The pivotal point in the war for him came in January 1945 when he was captured and taken prisoner. Bill was one of approximately 320 men who moved up to attack what intelligence said was a group of Germans about the same size as his group. But intelligence was wrong, and they were vastly outnumbered. Bill was a runner for the colonel, taking messages to and from the field HQ and the various outposts. He had always suspected that the Germans never shot at him so that they could see where he was going. The battle grew progressively worse, and the colonel repeatedly called HQ, asking permission to retreat. Repeatedly he was denied. Finally at about ten o'clock that night, he asked one last time. HQ once again told him to hold their position and said they would send up trucks with ammo and supplies. Bill says the colonel's reply is still seared in his brain: "Let the boys sleep, because we won't be here." The colonel then destroyed the radio. Shortly afterward their position was overrun. Out of the 320 men who started out, approximately 35 were left.

Everyone thought the Germans were just going to shoot them. Bill said he didn't care. "I was completely exhausted, thirsty, and hungry and had a slight shrapnel wound on my hand. I had made my peace and just didn't care what happened," he recalls. Instead, the Germans marched them off. Bill remembers stopping at the Rhine River. There had to be all sorts of pollution and bad stuff in the river, but Bill was so thirsty, he dunked his helmet in and drank. They then boarded a cattle car and traveled for three days and four nights. It was so packed that no one could sit down.

At the other end of this journey was Stalag 11B. This would be home for Bill for the next three and a half months until he was freed. They lived in spartan conditions. Their bunk beds were just sheets of plywood, measuring three feet wide, and there were two men to a bed. A single wood stove served as their heat source. They were given one bowl of watery soup a day and a two-inch square of bread. Bill later found the recipe for the bread and discovered that it was 30 percent sawdust. They never changed their clothes or showered once during their imprisonment.

Stalag 11B was considered one of the worst prisoner-of-war camps in Germany. Its prisoners came from a variety of countries: Russia, Serbia, Mongolia, etc. Bill slipped under the barbed wire into the Russian sector and got to know a Russian engineer. As they watched the B-17s fly overhead untouched, they knew the war had to be coming to an end. Bill said to the Russian engineer that he must be excited to be going home soon. The Russian replied that he could never return home, as he knew too much and would be shot. He also warned Bill that within five years America and the Soviet Union would be fighting each other. The Korean War broke out five years later.

The day the camp was liberated, Bill said it was as though it had been orchestrated by Hollywood. British tanks broke down the gates with a man—whom Bill later learned was the British general, Montgomery—standing on the first tank. Bill spent some time in a British hospital and then returned to the States.

Years later, Bill and his wife took the school band on a group tour of Europe. On a day off, they rented a car and drove to see whether they could find the place where Bill had been captured. He described to her the house, the barn, and some surrounding landmarks as they drove. Later, as they were walking in the area, his wife stopped and said, "Bill, there it is." Standing at the physical location made the memory of that fateful day very vivid.

Years later Bill ran into a former student who had been a POW in the Vietnam War. As they were talking about it, Bill told the man that he needed to put his wartime experiences behind him. The student told Bill that he didn't understand anything about survivor's guilt. Bill, a very mild-mannered man, raised his voice and told him of his own experiences—and about the flashbacks he had been having in the classroom at the very time when he had taught this student. The former student's parents later told Bill that that conversation had helped turn the man around and that he went on to lead a successful life.

Bill Funke

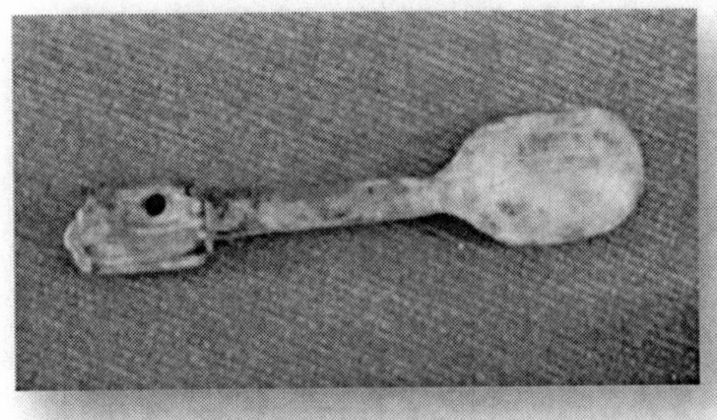

A spoon Bill carved out of a piece of wood so that he could eat.

Something to Prove

When he was growing up, Bernie Gaudreau always thought of himself as a failure. He really hadn't done much or accomplished anything. The reason for that was a leaky heart valve and the fact that Bernie had been told not to do any physical activity because of it. He could easily have sat out the war with a medical deferment because of his heart condition. But Bernie wanted to join, in part because he wanted to serve his country, but mainly because he wanted to prove something to himself. Once he had joined the military, he could have taken a desk job, but he was determined to be the best. He wanted to be in the Airborne.

The Airborne is one of the toughest programs, both mentally and physically, in the Army. They only take the best of the best, and even then many wash out. Bernie started out behind the eight ball in comparison to everyone else, but he excelled in the program, growing mentally and physically tougher throughout the training. He was now a member of the elite 101st Airborne.

The 101st shipped off to England and began training for what would become known as D-Day. On the evening of June 5, 1944, Bernie and the 101st boarded planes for the trip across the Channel to France. Their mission was to parachute inland to prevent German forces from making their way to the coast to repel the beach invasion that was planned for the next morning. The flight across the Channel to France was one that evoked both awe and terror for Bernie. Looking down at all the ships assembled for the invasion left him awestruck. The terror began as they crossed over the coast into France, and the Germans opened up with an antiaircraft barrage. Transport planes were being shot out of the sky. Bernie watched as the plane next to his was hit and then exploded. He would later learn that it was the plane he was initially supposed to be on but that he was pulled from because he was the radioman, in order to be with the commander, who was on a different plane. "I had gone the whole way through training and bunked with most of those on that plane," Bernie says with sadness.

Because of the chaos caused by the artillery barrage, many of the pilots turned on the jump light before they reached their designated jump zone. Bernie remembers floating down from the plane with tracer bullets, flak explosions, and burning planes all around him. The chaos continued on the ground, as men weren't at their designated landing points and often were not with their unit. They began forming up with whomever they came across. Each man had a small clicker with him, its clicking signal helping to separate friend from foe in the darkness.

The next morning Bernie was hit by a sniper while crossing a road. He managed to make it to cover behind a barn and pointed out to the others where he thought the shot came from. Bernie lay injured until the main forces arrived to secure the area, and he was medically evacuated. During the ambulance ride to the coast to catch a hospital ship back to England, he had a wrenching interaction with another soldier, the memory of which is still very emotional for him. Bernie tears up when he tells this part of the story. Lying across from him was a German soldier about his age, in severe pain, with his arm barely attached to his body. The road was rough and bumpy, so Bernie reached over and held the man's hanging arm so that it wouldn't fall off. The soldier looked at him with gratitude. "A half hour earlier we were trying to kill each other. We were both too young to be doing what we were doing," he says.

Bernie took a hospital ship back to England and was placed in a hospital to recover from his wound, but the horrors of war continued. The Germans were sending Buzz bombs to England. The Buzz bomb was an early version of today's long-range missile. It was shot from the Continent with a set amount of fuel, and it buzzed until it ran out of fuel and then fell from the sky. You were okay as long as you could hear the buzz, but once it went quiet, you knew you might be in trouble. A Buzz bomb hit the hospital one day. Because he was unable to move and seek shelter, all Bernie could do was pull the covers over his head and say some prayers. He would go on to make a full recovery and return home.

Bernie has very little good to say about his experiences—or really about war in general. There was one positive outcome, however. He came home both physically and mentally stronger, and with more confidence, than when he left home. He says he felt like he could do anything. He set out to prove something to himself, and he did.

Bernie Gaudreau

Transferable Skills

Before the war Joe Graham was a struggling insurance underwriter going to college at night. Like many in the thick of the Great Depression, he had had a hard time finding a job. He had finally gotten a job with an insurance company but was told that it offered no chance of a promotion or a raise and that after two years he would be let go. But at least it was a job. He worked hard and excelled at it, and he was offered a permanent position, got a raise, and began training as an underwriter. In 1941, however, he ran into another problem. The government instituted the prewar draft, and Joe's company wasn't taking any chances by promoting anyone of draft age. With his career stalled, Joe decided to volunteer and get his one year of service over with. He enlisted in June of 1941, reported in September, and Pearl Harbor was bombed in December. His one-year commitment now became open-ended.

Joe was in base training when Pearl Harbor was attacked. He was at the home of a nice local couple who would invite soldiers over for Sunday dinner. Everyone was around the table talking when Joe thought he heard something on the radio. Normally reserved and polite, he yelled, "Shut up and listen!" Joe finished training and was retained as an instructor. He jokes that he flunked basic training three times, as he was an instructor for three classes before being sent off to Officer Candidate School.

Now a commissioned officer, he was assigned to the 781st Tank Battalion. In the unit's first assignment, it played a civilian role. The government hadn't settled on a tank design, and Joe's unit was given forty different prototypes to test before reporting their findings. Interestingly, the model they recommended, which they felt was far superior to the others, was a diesel-powered model. The problem was that there wasn't the refinery capacity to produce enough diesel, so a gasoline model was chosen. A sad side note to this decision was that gasoline-powered tanks become fiery infernos when they are hit on the battlefield. Another interesting side note was that for Joe, having grown up in New Jersey and New York, a tank was the first thing he had ever driven. He jokes that he has driven as though he is driving a tank ever since.

The 781st consisted of a number of heavy-tank companies and one light-tank company, Co. D, which was made up of misfits and mess-ups. Needless to say, they performed poorly, and their commander couldn't control them. He was relieved of his duty, and Joe was given the command. Shortly after Joe took over, Co. D was sent to Canada to work with the Canadians to develop infantry tank attack strategies. He told his men that they would go up there and make our country proud. One of the men asked why Co. D had been chosen. Without really thinking, Joe said, "Because we are the best damn tank company in the whole US Army." What happened next still astonishes Joe. The men must have taken his words literally, because almost overnight this group of misfits became a top-notch company and would operate as one throughout the war.

After a successful stint in Canada, Co. D rejoined the 781st, and the battalion shipped out for Europe. They arrived in Marseille shortly after the invasion of southern France. Their equipment was lost along the way, and they were stuck for three weeks on a miserable, muddy hill awaiting new equipment. In an effort to boost morale, the battalion commander announced that there would be a contest to name the hill and that the winner would get a three-day pass. While announcing the winner at the end of the contest, the commander was red-faced mad when he saw that someone had submitted the name "Chicken Shit Hill, take the pass and stick it up your ass!" That incident still makes Joe laugh, as he is certain it was someone from Co. D who submitted the name.

The 781st moved north and entered the fighting outside of Lyon. Later, during the Battle of the Bulge in a position near the village of Bitche, France, the 781st was attached to the 100th Infantry Division. Because of their efforts defending and eventually liberating Bitche, the 100th coined themselves the "Sons of Bitche." Because the 100th respected the 781st so much, they coined them the "Honorary Sons of

Bitche." The fighting eased up until they reached the city of Heidelberg. There they met heavy resistance, including civilians coming at them with their bare hands and Molotov cocktails. Higher command decided to concentrate all their forces to break through this resistance. This left Co. D with seventeen tanks and a couple of miscellaneous companies to guard an area along the river five miles long.

Joe remembers the intense fear they experienced as a result of being so undermanned. Everyone was on edge, and one night an outpost came on the radio in a hushed voice to report that they thought they saw movement coming from the river. Joe told them to open fire as they saw fit and then listened to the distant battle rage. At daybreak, Joe drove up to check on them. When he arrived, he found no tracks or other signs in the mud and guessed that the shadows cast by moonlit apple tree branches must have looked like soldiers.

From this point on, it was easy for the 781st. They continued on through Austria, down to Italy, and back up to Austria, which was where they were stationed when the war in Europe ended. Joe and his company had fought their way across Europe for seven months with only three days off during the entire time. He only lost one man, a sergeant who was much loved by both Joe and his men.

With the war over, Joe and his unit began occupation duties in an Austrian village. Joe was—and will always be—proud of the men in his company, but one incident at the village left him momentarily ashamed of them. One day the mayor and the parish priest asked him to come to the church, where they showed him that someone had piled human bones on the altar. Joe had his officers collect the men in front of the church. Once they had gathered, Joe walked out of the church with the bones in his arms and stood there in silence for a few minutes. He told the men how ashamed he was. He said he wasn't going to do anything to the company as a whole but was leaving it up to the men to find out who had done this and take care of it themselves. It was later reported to him that the culprit was found and that the men had implemented their own brand of justice. That

Sunday after Mass, Joe went up to the pulpit and, using the German he had learned in college, he made a speech that he had practiced over and over, apologizing to the people of the village. The village, so accustomed to pompous German officers, was amazed that Joe was apologizing to them. His actions quickly put the issue to rest and added to the respect the village had for the Americans.

Joe looks back now on his military career with pride. He is also grateful for the skills that the Army and his experiences taught him. A struggling underwriter before the war, he returned to the insurance industry after the war, and, applying the skills of leadership, relationship building, operations, etc. that he learned during the war to a business context, he went on to have a highly successful forty-four-year career.

Joe Graham

A Lost Dream

Louis Hamman wanted to graduate from high school before going off to the service. By enlisting early and entering the Army's Specialized Training Program (ASTP), he was able to finish out his senior year. During this year, he won the state track title in the mile run and set his sights on trying out for the Olympics. He graduated on June 5 and shipped out with the Army on June 8. Approximately ninety-two of the one hundred male students from his high school class of 1943 would eventually leave for the service as well.

Louis first went to Texas for basic training and was then sent to New York City to begin ASTP. While there, he went to Jack Dempsey's restaurant and actually met the boxer. Louis told Jack that he had been born near the boxer's hometown. When he left, he was told that Jack had picked up his tab. Lou thought it was because of what he had told Jack, but he later learned that Jack quietly picked up the tab of any serviceman who patronized his place.

When the Army anticipated a shortage of infantryman, programs such as the ASTP were canceled, and everyone was sent to the infantry. Lou ended up in Co. E, 413th Infantry Regiment of the 104th Infantry Division. It was an interesting infusion into the 104th, since a ragtag outfit made up of many men who couldn't read or write was suddenly being joined by men coming from a program that required high test scores for admission.

After training, the 104th shipped out and headed directly to France and from there to Belgium, where they entered the fighting. Lou, trained as a scout and a sniper, was sent ahead to take out a German sniper. The sniper got a bead on him first and shot at him. Lou dived into the freezing water of a canal, where he had to stay until dark. When he got out, he walked to a burning house and went right into it to warm up.

His unit later came across a Dutch farmer crying after finding out that a horse he had kept hidden in his cellar had been killed. The men took a pair of German horses they had captured and gave him the team. He told them he couldn't take the pair because his neighbors knew he only had one horse. The men wrote out a letter stating that they were a gift from the US government and signed it "President Roosevelt."

As a scout, Lou was sent out to lead an eight-man patrol into enemy territory. They got the information they were looking for, but on the way back one of the men accidently hit the trip wire on a booby trap, and everyone was killed except Lou. He got back to HQ and gave the commander his report and then collapsed. The next thing he remembered was waking up in the hospital. His right leg was riddled with shrapnel, as was his face. The same day his mother received a telegram that Lou had been injured, she also got one informing her that Lou's brother was missing in action. It was a rough period for her until she learned that both her sons were okay. When Lou healed and returned to his unit, he only recognized the captain and five cooks. Everyone else had been wounded or killed. He was made a squad leader and given replacements for the men who had been lost.

The 104th, once a ragtag outfit, turned out to be a highly effective and decorated division, earning a Presidential Unit Citation. Lou himself was awarded the Bronze Star three times, as well as the Purple Heart.

Lou returned home and tried to pick up where he left off. He took up track again, renewing his aspirations of trying out for the Olympics, but his leg injury put an end to that dream. He still carries shrapnel in his leg and to this day is still picking shrapnel out of his forehead.

Louis Hamman

Unique Perspective

Walter Hotchkiss had the unique perspective of seeing Europe before, during, and after the end of the war.

Walter first went to Europe as a thirteen-year-old on a tour with a group of students. They spent a month visiting the Continent. He distinctly remembers their time in Berlin. "There were the red, black, and white Nazi flags and banners everywhere," he recalls. "But what I remember very well was that practically every man we saw as we toured the city was in a uniform." Five years later he would be back in Germany again, fighting his way toward Berlin.

Walter was in California at a boarding school when Pearl Harbor was bombed. He remembers the worry about a possible invasion of the West Coast by the Japanese. As soon as he graduated from high school, he was drafted into the Army. After basic training, he was put into a coastal artillery unit.

In 1944 Walter was transferred to the 417th Infantry Regiment of the 76th Infantry Division. The Army anticipated a shortage of infantrymen and needed bodies, so they started pulling men from anywhere and everywhere: pilot programs, officer training, etc.

After another round of basic training, Walter and the 76th shipped off to England, where they received still further training before crossing into France. While in England the men got passes to go into London. Since Walter had been there before, he acted as a tour guide, taking the men around to see the various sights.

Once on the Continent, Walter moved up to Luxembourg, and his unit set up beside the Saar River. It was one of the coldest winters in Europe's history, so they put up with extreme cold and deep snow. After a warm spell, the snow melted, and they discovered that strewn throughout the field where they were camped were dead bodies. Walter examined a dead German soldier and pulled out his wallet. In it was a picture of the man in his uniform with a proud look on his face and a woman hanging on his arm. Walter remembers telling another soldier, "Thank God she didn't see him like this." He put the wallet back in the pocket so the soldier could eventually be identified.

Soon the Americans began preparing to cross the river. Shallow wooden boats were brought to the front. On the night that the men picked up their boats and started down to the river, a lieutenant randomly pointed at Walter and told him to take some men and wait back at an abandoned house. This probably saved his life. The Germans began shooting at them and, with the river at flood stage, and the men laden down with equipment and ammunition, the boats overturned, and many men drowned, including a number of Walter's friends. He safely crossed the river the next day.

On his birthday Walter got what he considers one of the best presents he has ever received. The field doctor diagnosed him with early stages of pneumonia and put him on a hospital train to Paris. He rejoined his unit a few weeks later, but by now the Germans were in full retreat, and there was not much fighting. Walter remembers the stream of people coming in the opposite direction, trying to flee the Russians. All the soldiers really wanted to go all the way to Berlin, including Walter, who badly wanted to see it again, and they were disappointed when they were stopped short, in order to allow the Russians to take the city.

After the war, Walter would go on to a career in education. He became an adventurer and traveler as well, traveling to Europe many times. This gave him the third of his perspectives on Europe—the postwar rebuilding and modernization.

Walter Hotchkiss

Camping

Burl Huitt says he spent three months "camping" in a French forest during the war. Camping to him, but hiding from the Germans to the rest of us.

Burl's journey to his "campsite" began in England. He was a copilot on a B-24 with the 93rd Bomber Group. The crew started flying missions to the continent in April of 1944. After their fifth mission, their pilot came down with pneumonia and was taken off active duty. From this point on, the crew never flew with the same pilot, having a different one for every mission. They flew nine missions this way. Some of the pilots were good, but many were so bad that Burl often had to take over the controls. It got to the point that the crew became spooked, and they told Burl so. As the officer of the crew, Burl went to the commanding officer to express his and the crew's concerns. The CO agreed that he hadn't been fair to the crew and that Burl should take over as pilot. He told Burl to report back the next afternoon to take a test flight with him, and then the crew would be his.

Early the next morning Burl was roused out of bed and told he was flying that morning. Burl told the airman that there was some sort of mistake, as he had his test flight later that afternoon. The manifest listed him, though, so Burl reported to the briefing room, where he found that he was indeed flying, but not with his crew. In fact, he would never see his crew again. He was flying in the lead plane on a mission to Germany. Once Burl was in the plane, a colonel came up to the cockpit saying he wanted to fly. He wanted Burl to go back to the fuselage to keep an eye on the formation and giving him periodic updates.

As the formation approached its target, the weather grew progressively worse, and the mission was finally scrubbed. On the way back to England, the colonel spotted an air base in France and decided to bomb that instead. In return, antiaircraft artillery on the ground opened up on the planes. Up to this point, Burl had been lying on the floor, looking out a window at the formation and giving the colonel updates. The leg straps of his parachute had become uncomfortable, and he had unhooked them. All of a sudden he was kicked hard by one of the waist gunners. He looked up to see a wall of flames coming from the front of the plane. Flak had hit the bomb bay, killing everyone in the front of the plane. The two waist gunners immediately jumped out their windows. Burl stood up and tried to head back to warn the tail gunner. He also tried to reconnect the leg straps on his parachute. With the plane now fully engulfed in flames, however, the heat was so intense that he could do neither and instead jumped out of the plane himself.

Burl pulled the rip cord of his parachute, but with the leg straps not hooked, the parachute pack immediately flew off. Fortunately Burl was quick enough to grab it, but instead of being in the parachute pack, he was now dangling from it by his arms, straining with all his strength to hold on. He landed in the backyard of a farmhouse. A farmwife and her young daughter came out of the house and immediately gathered up his parachute. Noticing that his face was burned, she ran back into the house and came back out with some sort of yellow substance. She treated his face and pointed over to a field where he could hide. Burl ran and took cover in what he considered a well-hidden position in the field. Soon a man came up the road on a bike, and he stopped right where Burl was, gesturing for him to come out. Fortunately, he was part of the French Resistance and had come to take Burl to a safer place.

The safe place proved to be a camp in the middle of the forest. Burl was surprised when he arrived to find the two waist gunners and the tail gunner from his plane, whom he had attempted to save. They were the first in the camp, which would eventually swell to 150 airmen. For the next three months they hid in the forest camp, undetected by the Germans. They would go out at night on supply missions, assisted by the local farmers. Their conditions were actually quite comfortable, and Burl saw his sojourn in the forest as nothing more than an extended camping trip, much like the ones he had taken in the mountains of Colorado when he was growing up. Back home though, things weren't nearly so tranquil for his wife and his parents. For three agonizing months, after receiving a telegram from the Army that simply read, "We regret to inform you that Burl Huitt is missing in action. No other information at this time," they did not know whether he was alive or dead.

One of the amenities at the camp was a radio that provided the men with information on how the war was progressing. Trying to save the batteries, they only listened to the BBC news for a short period of time at night, but they were aware of the D-Day landings. A couple of weeks later, as they heard radio reports about the progression of the Allies, three members in the camp decided it was time to try to head west to get help. They hadn't gotten too far from camp when they came across an American tank unit. The tankers radioed back for help, and the camp occupants were soon picked up and back on the friendly side of the front lines. The first chance he got, Burl sent a message home. Both his simple telegram saying, "Don't worry, all is well," and the Army's, saying, "Pleased to announce that Burl Huitt has returned to active duty," arrived at his parent's house at the same time.

Burl always felt fortunate about his experience—fortunate that he wasn't up in the cockpit that day and that he spent the time in the forest instead of a German POW camp. Many years later he returned to France to find the location of the camp and possibly some of the locals who had helped him, but he found neither. Because many of the forests in France were not natural, but rather planted by people, he speculates that the forest in which he hid had been harvested at some point. The forest, which witnessed both human good and human evil, no longer exists to tell the tale.

Burl Huitt

Investment Pays Off

Thirty-nine cents and a pocket knife. That was the price Dale Hunter paid for his first airplane ride as a twelve year old. A pilot landed in a neighbor's field in Rice County, Kansas, and told Dale that he would give him a ride for whatever he had in his pocket. After Dale turned over his life savings and took the ride, he was hooked on aviation.

After the war broke out, Dale wanted to be a pilot, but he knew that because he wore glasses, he would never be accepted. He enlisted in the Army Air Corps anyway and became a mechanic in the 731st Bomb Squad, 452nd Bomber group of the 8th Air Force. After zigzagging around the country for training, he shipped off to Europe. He traveled to England on the *Queen Elizabeth* ocean liner, which had been converted to a troop ship.

In England, the 452nd set up operations at Deopham Green air base, where Dale worked on B-17 bombers. The planes flew missions during the day, and the ground crews worked on them at night. Each ground crew was assigned to take care of a specific plane. The 8th Air Force took horrendous losses during this time; Dale took care of seven different airplanes while he was there, and six of those planes never returned to base. The crews were either killed or became POWs when those planes went down. "It was sad to look up in the sky in the afternoon as the formations came back from a mission and not see your plane return," Dale recalls.

While Dale and the ground personnel at the base were obviously much safer than the air crews, they were not always out of harm's way. Twice they got bombed by the Germans. Another time a fire started in the hangar and soon consumed the plane Dale was working on.

When he was granted furloughs, Dale often spent them traveling around England. He became acquainted with an English farm family and spent many of his furloughs with them. He gave his ration coupons to the wife and helped the husband with farm chores. He wrote home to his dad, asking him to send some Milo seed so the farmer could try a new type of feed for his cattle.

When the war ended in Europe, Dale returned home with a thirty-day leave. His orders called for him then to report to South Dakota, where he would be transferred into the infantry and sent to the Pacific. All along the way, on the train ride up, they passed people waving and screaming. At one of the stops, the conductor got off the train and discovered that the Japanese had surrendered.

Once Dale's service was up, he returned home and married Lila. They have been married for more than sixty-five years and have two children, three grandchildren, and four great-grandchildren. Dale went on to have a long career, primarily in the aviation industry. His and Lila's work took them all over the country, as well as to South America and Africa.

That investment Dale made as a kid sparked an interest that in turn gave him the opportunity to travel the United States and the world and to serve his country in the military.

Dale Hunter

Prays for the Fallen

"You don't have to kill a man to kill him." Joe Hoberman makes this profound statement when describing what he saw on his very first day on the front line. Joe says being in the war dramatically changed his life and that he constantly thinks about those who didn't make it back.

Joe turned eighteen early in his senior year of high school and took extra classes so he could graduate in January instead of the spring. Based on his high test scores, he then enlisted in the Army's Specialized Training Program. He learned how to code and decode messages, but, anticipating a shortage of infantryman, the Army ended the program and transferred everyone to the infantry. Sent to the European Theater, Joe landed in Normandy as a replacement. While hiking up and over the hills at Omaha Beach on the way to the repo depot, he noted how steep a climb it was and wondered what it must have been like for those who had to fight their way up it. Once at the replacement depot—or, as the soldiers called it, the "repple depple"—he was assigned to the 3rd Infantry Division.

Joe experienced the horrors of war on his very first day on the front line. During a German artillery barrage, the headquarters was wiped out. The rest of the unit sought refuge in a ravine during the barrage, and once it was over, Joe and another soldier were ordered to recover whatever important documents they could from the remains of the fallen. They came across a gruesome sight. All the officers had been killed. They came across one survivor, a thirty-six-year-old they affectionately called "Pop." "He was completely out of it mentally. We guided him out of there as you would a total invalid," Joe says. "I have always wondered whatever became of him." It was this experience that prompted Joe to say, "You don't have to kill a man to kill him."

Horrible experiences continued to stack up for Joe in short order. His best friend, Ernie, was killed on their second day out. This left Joe scared to death, but he now realizes that being scared makes for a great defense. With his extremely keen senses, he was soon made a scout. Out on a recon mission with another scout, they got caught in a tree burst—a maneuver where the Germans lowered their guns into the trees, shattering them and showering the men in the forest with splintered pieces. The other scout's leg was severed by falling pieces of wood.

Joe was soon temporarily knocked out of the war himself. On the southern edge of the Battle of the Bulge and not properly outfitted for what was one of the coldest winters in Europe in fifty years, Joe's feet froze, and gangrene set in. He spent a month in the hospital recovering and then rejoined his unit. The war was now on German soil, and Joe remembers an experience that stopped him in his tracks. While raiding a house, he looked up at the writing on a grandfather clock. Fluent in German, he read, "One of these hours will be your last." Fortunately it was a prediction that didn't hold true at the time, and he survived the war.

With Germany's surrender, Joe was pressed into duty because of his earlier training in decoding messages. He went with American officers to meet a German field marshal to accept his surrender; Joe's skills would come in handy in case they needed to send off classified messages. When they returned, Joe was hauled into his commanding officer's office and told he was now subject to a court martial. Stumped, Joe asked what he had done. The officer said that Joe had not saluted the German field marshal. "I absolutely would not!" Joe declared to the officer. The officer walked up to him, smiled, and said he was excused. Joe stayed in Germany for a year after the war ended as part of the occupation forces until he finally had enough points to come home.

While he is very proud of his service and of being part of the 3rd Infantry Division, Joe doesn't like to talk about the war and sees no good in doing so. Aside from the nightmares, which have only stopped in recent years, he tries not to think about it, either. Fair enough, on both counts, after all he went through. He can't stop thinking about those who never made it back, though. "I pray several times a week for my friends who never made it back," he says with sorrow that, seventy years later, is still strong in his voice.

Joe Hoberman

Farm, War, and History

Howard Johnston was a tough farm boy from Nebraska when he went off to war. An agricultural deferment kept him on the farm until after harvest, and then he was off to basic training. The fact that he had just having finished the hard work of the harvest gave Howard an edge over those in his class. He and another recruit were the only two of the entire company to finish the first big hike during their training. On the next hike, he once again arrived first, carrying someone's pack and three others' rifles along with his. He also proved to be the ace shot of the class. Once when a soldier was holding up the entire class because he couldn't get qualified with his rifle, the drill sergeant told Howard to set up at the station next to this soldier and pick off his target, getting the soldier qualified. Basic training proved to be easy for Howard.

Basic training was cut short, though, as the Battle of the Bulge began, and soldiers were needed on the front lines. Everyone was hurried to the East Coast and put on the *Queen Mary* for England. They departed for Europe on Howard's twentieth birthday. They landed in Scotland, took a train down to southern England, and were immediately put on a transport to the French coast. Howard arrived at the front line as a replacement for Co. C, 314th Infantry Regiment of the 79th Infantry Division. When he arrived, the company was so shot up that it was at 50 percent capacity. Although he was a green replacement, Howard quickly fit in and began to do his part. His foxhole buddy was Bill, who was the first scout. Howard became second scout, and together they began running recon missions ahead of the company. Howard explains that he has been able to put this horrible and frightening time on the front lines behind him, except for one incident that still bothers him. He and Bill were out on recon, walking on either side of a street through a village, when Bill motioned up to a second-story window where a rifle was sticking out. Howard ran across the road and threw a grenade into the window. They both rushed the house, broke down the door, and went upstairs to find that the grenade had killed a ten-year-old boy and his mother. Howard realizes that this incident happened in the thick of war, and he was in a situation where it was "kill or be killed," but it bothers him nonetheless.

The 79th fought into Germany. They had crossed the Rhine and were helping to clear out the Ruhr pocket when the war came to an end. After three months on the front lines, the fighting was over for Howard. What happened next for him put him into the middle of another significant historical event. He was pulled from the 79th to become a guard during the Nuremburg Trials. During this time, he guarded Hermann Goering and Julius Streicher. Howard says that, setting aside the fact that he was a monster, Goering was polite to him. He also managed to get Streicher's signature, which he still keeps as a memento. He spent time inside the actual trial as well, but it was during the segment that the French presided over, and it was thus hard for him to follow. After his stint at the trials, he returned to his unit and began performing duties in the occupation forces until he acquired enough points to go home.

His return home was an emotional experience for everyone. Mustered out at Fort Riley, he started hitchhiking to Nebraska. He was picked up by a pair of old women who bought him dinner and then by a truck driver who took him as far as the town where one of Howard's older brothers lived. He had not yet been able to tell anyone that he was coming come. His brother was over the moon that he was home and quickly came to get him. He then called ahead to their parents to tell them that he would bring Howard home later that day. Their mother broke down crying upon hearing the news and couldn't stop. Howard's best buddy—his hunting dog—must have sensed what was happening, as he ran up the road to a hill above the farmhouse and began howling. He stayed up there howling the entire day until Howard arrived and then knocked him over and jumped all over him, licking his face, when he got out of the car.

Like many of his generation, Howard put his wartime experiences behind him and moved on with his life. He would go on to have a career in retail, was married to his wife Evelyn for sixty-five years until she passed away, and raised three children. He really didn't think about war experiences much again until he was on a vacation with his family in southern California. They went to Long Beach and were going on a tour of the *Queen Mary* for his birthday. It hit him then that he was boarding the ship sixty-eight years to the day after he had left for war. Howard expresses a sentiment many of his fellow veterans share: "I would never want to do it again, but I wouldn't trade a million dollars for the experience."

Howard Johnston

Coming Full Circle

The minute he learned about paratroopers on the newsreels at the movie house, Stan Kass knew that was what he wanted to be. He enlisted in the Army, did his basic training in New Jersey, and then shipped off to Ft. Benning, Georgia, for paratrooper training. Although it was a very difficult and vigorous program, Stan loved it—and thrived on it.

After successfully completing the program and earning his Parachutist Badge or jump wings, Stan became part of the 508th Parachute Infantry Regiment of the 82nd Airborne. The 82nd soon set sail for Europe, landing in England, where they continued to train for the upcoming invasion.

On June 5, 1944, the 82nd began assembling and preparing to take off for France ahead of the main invasion force. There is a famous picture of General Eisenhower talking to men from the various airborne divisions out on the tarmac. The first man on the left, wearing a helmet, is Stan. The paratroopers loaded up and took off for Normandy that night. Flying across the Channel, he had the feeling he was going to die, and he says he was lucky that he didn't take any ground fire while parachuting out of the plane. He remembers the awful sight of burning planes going down around him.

Given the general chaos and the fire from the ground, the operation was disorganized. Most units landed far from their designated landing zones. The purpose of the night jumps was to keep additional Germans from getting to the landing beach and then to begin fighting their way to the beaches. When they finally linked up with the invasion forces the next day, their job was done, and they returned to England. Stan figures that about half his unit was lost.

The 82nd then trained and prepared for its next jump, which was a daytime jump into Holland and Germany in September, which was known as Operation Market Garden. This was the largest airborne operation to date, with the objective of getting across the Rhine River. Stan remembers landing in the morning and enjoying a leisurely breakfast, and then suddenly the Germans were on top of them. The operation proved to be unsuccessful, and the Allies were unable to cross the Rhine.

The 82nd then set up camp in France. When the Battle of the Bulge broke out, they were taken by truck to the battle. Stan laughs as he remembers everyone jumping out of the back of the trucks yelling "Geronimo!" They were not dressed properly for the cold weather and suffered miserably. Stan still deals with the aftereffects of having had frozen feet. The Allies finally turned the tide and broke through, and the front lines started moving quickly toward Berlin. By this time, Stan had enough points and was sent back to the States and discharged. He reenlisted and returned to Ft. Benning to teach new recruits. Altogether he made twenty-eight jumps.

Stan very much wanted to return to Germany, as he loved the land and the people. He went back as part of the occupation forces and was assigned to be the driver for a general. There was only one problem: having grown up in Brooklyn, he had never learned to drive. He told the general's assistant that before he took the assignment, he had to take care of some business. He left for a week and went off to learn how to drive. Later, in an ironic twist of fate, as the senior driver in the carpool, he was assigned to drive General Eisenhower! He had flown through the air for this general and was now driving for him.

Stan Kass with his brothers

Stan is the first one in the helmet from the left.

A Soldier's Best Friend

"Next to God, a soldier's best friend is the medic." This famous quote could not describe Bob Korth better. Bob served as a medic in WWII with the 104th Infantry Division, "the Timberwolves." Bob and the Timberwolves entered the war a week after D-Day in Cherbourg, France, and fought their way across Europe until they drank vodka with the Russians at the Elbe River in Germany at the war's end.

Bob was born in Canada to Swedish immigrant parents. His family finally settled in Los Angeles, where he excelled in many sports. He would be drafted into the Army twice. The first time was during the prewar draft, and he was soon released with a medical discharge. Despite the medical discharge, he was drafted again in 1942. With no medical background and very little training, it was trial by fire as Bob learned everything about being a medic on the battlefield.

The combat medic often risked his life, and many times sacrificed it, while coming to the aid of an injured or sick comrade. Bob was no exception to this. He was wounded twice while coming to the aid of wounded soldiers and twice received the Purple Heart. He was also awarded the Bronze Star twice for his bravery. In one of these instances he went into the crossfire of two German machine gun nests to pull injured soldiers to safety. The citation that came with one of his Bronze Stars read in part, "At great risk to his life he made numerous trips across open fire-swept terrain under direct enemy fire in order to evacuate casualties . . . in spite of the enemy fire he continued to perform his duties in a superior manner . . . his courageous actions saved the lives of many of his comrades." Bob often rendered aid to a soldier on the battlefield and then took him by stretcher for distances of miles back to the aid station, only to turn around and do it over and over again. He often encountered numerous obstacles, once crossing a canal totally submerged while holding an injured officer high over his head to keep him dry.

The Timberwolves remained in continuous frontline battle for 195 consecutive days from Holland to Germany—the most of any division during the war. Along the way they liberated Nordhausen concentration camp. In the chaos of the destroyed German infrastructure and services, Bob also delivered the baby of a German woman. It was a skill that would come in handy when he later helped deliver one of his own daughters!

Returning home after the war, Bob met and married Edna, who had been his pen pal during his time overseas. They spent sixty-two years together and had four children, six grandchildren, and three great-grandchildren. After returning from the war, he also began what would be a thirty-five-year career in civil service.

To know Bob was to know a very kind and gentle man. These characteristics must have brought additional comfort to the wounded soldiers he took care of. Bob passed away a couple of years ago. A soldier's two best friends are now together.

Bob Korth

The Soldier and the Little Girl

War is hell. That statement is a cliché, but those of us who have never experienced it can never truly understand it. It is something, however, that World War II veteran Roy Laman understands very well. Roy is the first to admit that he was lucky and that he had it better than the front line soldier. As a communications officer with the 2nd Signal Battalion who processed top secret messages, he jokes that he was close enough to the front line not to have to wear a tie, but far enough back not to be shot at. But as Roy and his unit followed the war across Europe, he saw the results of war: the destruction, the death and maiming, the desperate people along the roads begging for food. I can see in his eyes and in his voice that sixty-five years later, this still bothers him very much. As he is describing his wartime experiences, he tells me about a three-week period when he received a wonderful reprieve from it all.

This period of very fond memories started for Roy when his unit pulled into Herleen, Holland, to set up their headquarters. He was billeted with a local family and soon became very close to them—one of the young daughters, Irmine, in particular. "They were incredibly kind to me and the other soldier staying there and treated us like members of the family," he recalls. One memory that stands out was the warm feeling and sense of family he was missing but that he experienced when he went to Christmas Eve services with the family. He and Irmine played games and took walks. He brought them supplies when he could. He laughs when he describes once bringing cans of sweet corn and being stumped by their reaction. He soon found out that In Holland corn was only eaten by livestock. Chocolate, on the other hand, was like gold to them. As the front line started moving east toward Germany, it was time for Roy to move on as well. While saying his good-byes to the family, Irmine's sister Illa presented him with a braid of hair. She had cut it off to give him a memento to remember them all by. Roy carried that braid with him through the rest of the war. Sadly, however, an outbreak of scabies on the troop ship heading home after the war had ended forced everyone to toss all their personal items overboard, and the braid of Illa's hair went into the sea along with everything else. While his mother sent the family packages shortly after the war, Roy eventually lost touch with the family.

The evening of my interview with Roy, as I was processing his videotaped interview in order to give the tape back to him and his family, I couldn't stop thinking about this story. I have done many interviews, and almost every one of them has had an effect on me. Roy's story was no exception, the only difference being that this time it was a happier story. I tossed and turned in bed that night, thinking about it. I could tell from the sparkle in Roy's eyes just how special this time and this family were to him. Like many of the other stories I have heard in the past, it seeped into my dreams. When I woke up the next morning, I decided I had to try to find Irmine.

Finding Irmine proved to be easy—a testament to the power of the Internet. I didn't have her last name or an address, but I did have pictures. Without telling Roy what I was doing, I found the Website of the local newspaper in Herleen. Plugging words into a translation feature, I worked my way around the newspaper's site until I found their "news tips" button. I sent them a message explaining what I was trying to do and asked whether they could help. A week went by with no response, and I began to wonder what other approaches I could take. I then received an e-mail from Stefan Gillisson, a reporter with the newspaper, saying he would be interested in doing such a story. We exchanged additional e-mails in which I gave him what details and pictures I had. He said the story would run the following Saturday. Friday night I tossed and turned in bed as I had the night after I first interviewed Roy. Finally, very early in the morning, I got up and turned on the computer. Given the time difference between the Netherlands and Colorado, I hoped there would be good news, and in fact there was an e-mail from Stefan saying that Irmine had been found!

Soon afterward I got an e-mail from Irmine's neighbor Frank. Because she read in the article about how much that Christmas Eve service meant to Roy, Frank and Irmine went over and snapped a picture of her in front of the church and e-mailed it to me. I received a number of e-mails from others as well. What struck me about every e-mail I received was that each one mentioned how grateful they still were for what the Americans had done. I waited for a decent hour to call Roy and his wife, Marilyn. I then took all the e-mails and the picture of Irmine over to them. I also took my video camera. They recorded a message to Irmine, and I sent it to her via YouTube. A few days later Irmine and Frank replied with a video message. The story only grew more special and touching once Irmine told her side of it.

When Stefan did a follow-up article, Irmine pulled out her wartime diary and showed him the message Roy had written in it:

To my little darling. Of all the girls in the world, you have made me most happy. You

see, I have a little darling [a special niece] *back in America. While I am in Holland, you have*

been like that little girl. I hope you will grow up to be a grand lady like your mother. May

you always be happy and stay as beautiful as you are today. Love you baby. Yours, Roy

She talked about the games they played and the walks they took. She also described the time Roy announced that a great American general had come to their town. Irmine's mother wrapped a red, white, and blue shawl around her, and she and Roy walked hand in hand to go meet the general. She sat on the general's lap, and he gave her a bag of donuts. As a little girl, she had had no idea who General Eisenhower was.

Roy returned home after the war, went into the printing business, and married Marilyn. They have been married for sixty-four years and had five sons (one of whom, sadly, died in an auto accident), nine grandchildren, and one great-grandchild. Irmine went on to start a program in the Netherlands that helps children in Third World countries. She had been married to her husband, Peter, for forty-five years until his death six months earlier. In the follow-up article Irmine said, “I miss Peter very much. Roy’s search comes at the right moment. It lightens my heart and eases the sadness.”

We made an effort to try to plan a visit for Roy and Irmine, but Roy was now in his nineties and too feeble to travel, and Irmine was terrified of flying. An intense correspondence between these two old friends did develop, though. Sadly, however, only few months after she and Roy had reconnected, Irmine was diagnosed with a brain tumor, and she passed away within weeks of the diagnosis.

Irmine and Roy

The Love of Flying

Jack Lange acquired the flying bug at an early age. When he was a kid, and an airshow came to town, he would show up the day before or early on the day it opened and somehow finagle a ride with the pilots. In high school he realized that flying was what he wanted to do, and after graduating at age seventeen, he left his home in western Pennsylvania for an aviation school in California.

Jack's goal was to get into the Army Air Corps, but at the time recruits had to be twenty-one to fly, so he took a job as a draftsman with an aviation company. When the war broke out, he was anxious to join, but because he was working in a war-related industry, the company wouldn't let him go. So he quit his job, enlisted, and went home to wait to be called up.

Once he was drafted, Jack got his wings and trained as a B-25 pilot. The two closest calls he had while in the service came before he even made it to the war zone. The first occurred while he was lying in a formation during an inspection over the base. The planes in the formation ahead of him collided, and he and his formation pulled out just in time not to be involved. The second time was when his unit was shipping overseas to Europe to enter the war. They were an hour out of Newfoundland when an engine seized up. They were told to prepare for a possible water landing, and Jack knew they would never last in the cold north Atlantic waters. Fortunately the plane made it back to Newfoundland, but no sooner had they landed when the engine caught fire. Fire trucks met the plane at the runway, and they had to evacuate the plane.

Eventually the plane was repaired, and they continued their journey, going first to Scotland—skirting England because of the continuing German air raids—and down to Africa, then across to Italy where Jack would start flying missions. The air base he was supposed to go to was at the base of Mt. Vesuvius, which had erupted a couple of weeks earlier, destroying a number of planes and forcing the base to move farther south, out of harm's way. Jack flew a couple of missions that took him over the still active volcano, and he was able to look down into it as ash and smoke spewed out of it.

Jack's missions then came fast and furious. In a six-month period, he would fly fifty-eight missions. One of them was bombing the abbey at Cassino—part of the Allies' attempt to push the Germans out of this strategic hilltop location. The rest of his missions were a mixture of milk runs (easy missions) and harrowing ones, like the time when the wingmen on either side of him were shot out of the sky. The B-25 is a midlevel bomber and was mostly used to bomb bridges, marshaling yards, and highways in order to interrupt the movements of the German army. Jack flew most of these missions out of a base on the island of Corsica, where his unit, the 487th Bomb Squadron of the 340th Bomber Group, was transferred.

Jack was only required to fly fifty missions before going home, but he stayed on to fly another eight because he wanted to be part of the invasion of southern France. Finally rotating back to the States, he was sent to Arizona and Texas as an instructor until he was discharged.

Once he was out of the service, Jack continued his dream of having a career in aviation. He began by flying as a corporate pilot for a few years. During this time he met a woman named Sandy, who was getting her pilot's license, and he offered to help her with a portion of her training. She ultimately became his wife. He subsequently built an airport in his hometown and operated it for five years. This—the crown jewel of his aviation career—was followed by his thirty years with United Airlines. After retiring, Jack built an award-winning plane and is presently building another. He retired from United flying the large DC-10—a far cry from that small, open-cockpit plane he first flew in as a young boy.

Jack Lange

One Tough Cookie

Don Lawless is a very tough and determined man. Even though he is ninety and half my size, I wouldn't mess with him. He shows me an article about the time he and his wife were in Paris and were mugged by a group of kids, who stole his wallet. He beat up the whole lot of them and got his wallet back. He was sixty years old then. I can only imagine what he was like as a nineteen-year-old flying a P-47. His story clearly spells that out.

When the war broke out, Don wanted to get into the Air Corps. He had never been in an airplane but knew he wanted to fly. He also knew he didn't want to be on the ground. He remembers listening to his two uncles' stories about being in the trenches during World War I, and he wanted no part of that. He was accepted into the flying program and did exceedingly well. He received his wings and shipped off to Europe.

His group of replacement pilots arrived in Naples and from there he and sixteen others went on to the Island of Corsica to begin flying missions in a P-47 Thunderbolt, also known as a "flying tank" because of all the armaments on it. The primary mission of the P-47 was to fly low-level close support for the ground troops. They would attack tanks, trains, and artillery installations. Don says that, flying that low and close, his planes would often return to base perforated. There were three planes that he managed to bring back to base but that were incapable of being flown again. Once on a solo mission to do weather recon for a group of bombers, he couldn't resist dropping down to wreak havoc on a German air base on his way home. His unit moved with the war, eventually locating to front-line bases in France. While in France, Don ended up where he vowed he would never be, in a foxhole. A unit of British troops was bogged down along a stretch of the front lines by the Germans. Don spent some time embedded with them as a forward observer, helping call in dive-bombing airstrikes.

Don flew 101 missions in eleven months. He was a damn good pilot, at age twenty becoming the youngest flight leader in history. He was also damn lucky. Of those seventeen replacement pilots who set out together, Don would be the only one to survive the war unscathed. Twelve were killed and the other four injured severely enough to be taken out of the war. Don says he fully expected to be killed at some point. He made it through the war without a scratch, however, and only remembers one close call. A 20 ml shell from a tank hit his plane and ricocheted around in the cockpit, just barely missing him. Don finishes this story with an ornery grin, saying the tank paid the price for doing that.

Don was only required to fly fifty missions, but he wanted to keep on going. It took intervention by the major general of the flight group to make him stop at 101. Even then, he argued with the general to allow him to continue flying. Finally grounded and with enough points, he was allowed to go home: he laughs at an incident surrounding his return. A fellow pilot from his hometown of Wichita, who was in his flight group, but not his squadron, stopped over at his tent upon hearing the news that Don was going home. He showed Don a picture of his fiancée and asked Don to check on her when he got home. Don did, and six months later she and Don were married! He says it isn't as bad as it sounds, as the prior engagement had been prearranged by their mothers, and neither one really wanted it.

Don says he looks back on the war with fondness and realizes that, while this probably isn't the right thing to say, he enjoyed participating in the war and is very proud of his involvement. He went to all the unit's reunions throughout the years, eventually being its sole surviving member. He says his war experience taught him decision making, strategizing, and assertiveness, skills that he says he would eventually parlay into a very successful career in the oil industry. He is, and was, one tough cookie whom I am glad we were fortunate to have on our side.

Don Lawless

Old Country, New Country

George LeFever was the firstborn child of a hardworking immigrant couple from Belgium. His parents had already been affected by war in many ways. His father served stateside in World War I, which gave him his citizenship. It is also why their last name is what it is. During roll call the drill sergeant barked out "LeFever," and George's dad didn't answer. When he was the last person remaining in the group, he looked at the sergeant's clipboard and saw that LeFever would be a lot easier to say and spell in America than the Belgium spelling of his name—Laver'ge—so he changed it. Meanwhile, in Belgium George's mom, uncle, and grandmother were fleeing their village, which was being shelled by the Germans. George's grandfather stayed behind to guard their house and was killed by a shell.

Fast-forward a generation to 1941 and the bombing of Pearl Harbor. George was fourteen and far from old enough to serve. The family became part of the crucial home-front effort, raising crops and rotating them to help fill the needs of the nation. When there was a shortage of sugar, for example, they switched to growing sugar beets. When George turned seventeen, he desperately wanted to enlist. He asked his mother to sign the papers, and she told him to ask his father. "I didn't even bother, as it would have been like talking to a tree," George says, knowing that his father needed him on the farm. When he turned eighteen, though, the draft notice came, and George left for the Army.

Going off to the Army was an exciting experience for George. He saw other parts of the country and met people from these different regions. Because of the physical life he lived growing up on the farm, basic training was a breeze for him, unlike some of the city boys. George was in basic training when the atomic bombs were dropped, and the war ended. Soon after, he and another soldier were given notice to report to Army Counter Intelligence Corps (CIC) school at Camp Holabird, Maryland. They were given no other information. When they reported in, the officer asked them whether they knew how they got there. Lacking any information and not truly understanding the question, George's buddy answered, "Well, by train, sir." The officer swiveled his chair to hide his laughter at the answer and their naïveté. He swung around again and said, "You two were selected because you scored extremely high on testing." The officer soon discovered a problem, though: you have to be twenty-one to serve in the CIC, and neither George nor his buddy was that age yet. The Army decided to keep them in reserve and sent George to cooking school. He finished out his enlistment as a cook at the camp. One of his many memories of that time is the last Thanksgiving at the camp. As the lead cook, he and his assistant cook, along with two German POW helpers, cooked forty-eight turkeys for fifteen hundred personnel.

Via a connection at the camp, George was asked whether he would like to cook at the Waldorf Hotel in New York after his enlistment ended. While the idea intrigued this farm boy from Colorado, he declined and returned home to become a successful farmer. Like his father before him, in the previous war, George served Stateside in this war. Fortunately the men and women who served in this war assured that he—and this country—would never share the experiences of his mother's family.

George Lefever

Putting Images of War in the Past

What sticks out most when listening to Frank ("Sam") MacDonald talk about his experiences in World War II is everything that he saw.

After basic training Sam was sent to the Army Specialized Training Program. This elite program is hard to get into, as you must possess a high IQ. Unfortunately the Army projected a shortage of regular combat soldiers shortly after he entered, and it canceled Sam's program. Most everyone in the program was then sent to the 84th Infantry Division at Camp Claiborne, Louisiana. He was put into the 334th Infantry Regiment, 3rd Battalion, Co. I of the 84th.

After basic training, they shipped out to Europe and entered into combat in November 1944. On that first day, Sam was one of three men in a twelve-man unit who was not injured or killed. They immediately became the leaders and were given nine replacements. By drawing straws, Sam became the assistant squad leader. All three were privates who were just eighteen or nineteen years old.

On Christmas Day during the Battle of the Bulge, Sam's unit was overrun by the Germans. As a German tank fired its machine gun toward Sam, he dived into a foxhole. He felt a pain in his leg and figured he had landed on a shovel. He soon discovered that he had been shot. The Germans continued their advance, and for a week Sam and his men were trapped. They shivered in their foxholes during one of the coldest winters in Europe's history, boiled tree bark for food, and drank melted snow. A counteroffensive eventually freed them. From there they continued on to Holland where their squad leader was killed, instantly making Sam the squad leader. He would be the leader from then until they reached the Elbe River at the war's end.

Throughout the war he saw many sights:

–The carnage during battles, which he doesn't care to talk about.

–The German rockets in the sky heading to England. In reverse, the sky filled with thousands of Allied planes heading to Germany.
–A German jet fighter strafing their convoy. Everyone was terrified because they had never seen a jet before.
–The site where the Nazis took two thousand political prisoners, locked them into a barn, and set the barn on fire. The Army made a man from each unit come to witness this and go back to tell their unit about it. Sam was picked to go from his unit.
–The waves during a storm on the trip home. On the crest of the wave, the ship's propeller was out of the water, and while in the trough, the walls of water around them were seventy feet high. It was as terrifying as any of the battles.
–The Statue of Liberty and watching the ship list to the side as the men rushed to that side of the ship to see it.
–The cities and towns as he traveled across the United States to Colorado after the war. After seeing nothing but total destruction in Europe, he had a very hard time comprehending the sight of unscathed cities.

Of the 184 men who left Camp Claiborne with Sam, he would be one of only thirteen who made it the entire way through the war. He was awarded the Bronze Star and received the Purple Heart.

Sam has a jovial and upbeat personality. "I feel lucky that I had the ability to put behind what I saw and only concentrate on the good things that have happened in my life," he says. That ability is a good thing, because, like many in the war, Sam saw more than any person should ever have to.

Sam MacDonald

Falling from the Sky

Norm Markel's story centers around a number of "firsts" and one very important "last."

Norm enlisted in the Army Air Corps while still in high school. Once he graduated, he shipped off to cadet training school. He was the first in his family to fly on an airplane. His training would have him zigzagging all over the country. On one of his first training flights, he and his instructor flew into a snow cloud in Montana and got lost. Eventually they spotted a country landing strip where they brought their plane down. They spent the night in an old shack with a potbelly stove, and in the morning they brushed the snow off the plane and returned to base.

Norm was like many during this time who had the rug pulled out from under them when the Army announced it had enough pilots and was no longer training any more. He transferred to become a radioman and waist gunner. After additional training, Norm found himself in Lincoln, Nebraska, where he would meet up with his crew.

Norm remembers vividly the day he met his crew. It was a very hot and sunny day, and thousands of men were standing in a field as the base commander announced the crews. He was doing so in a slow, droning manner, and the uncomfortable conditions were making the men irritable. Finally someone in the crowd yelled, "Give me liberty or give me death!" The commander looked up from his list and yelled angrily, "Who said that?" From somewhere else in the crowd, another voice yelled back, "Patrick Henry, you dumb son of a bitch!" The place exploded with laughter, and it took a good twenty minutes for everyone to settle down again. Norm himself is laughing hard after he tells the story, but once he stops laughing, he closes his eyes and rattles off the names of his crew as the commander would have.

He and his crew began training together in what were pretty dangerous conditions. Given the combination of inexperience and worn-out planes, an average of one plane a week was crashing. Norm called his mother once a week just to reassure her that he was okay and not in one of the planes that had crashed.

Finally it was time to ship off for war. They left by train from Lincoln for the East Coast, where they caught a ship to England. On Christmas Eve the train passed through Norm's hometown, Michigan City, Indiana. He will tell you that looking out the window as the train passed through was one of the hardest things he has ever experienced, including what was yet to come!

The Atlantic crossing was uneventful, and Norm and his crew settled in at their base in Nuthampstead, England. They were now with the 8th Air Force's 398th Bomb Group, 602nd Bomb Squadron. They began flying training missions and soon took off to fly their first mission to the Continent. After they made their bombing run, the formation turned one way, and Norm's plane turned the other way. They were now lost and soon were running low on fuel. The pilot gave the order to prepare to bail out. Norm looked out the window, and in a break in the clouds, he noticed land. He told the pilot, and the pilot said he better be right, since they would not have enough fuel to climb back up again. Once below the clouds, they came across a bombed-out airfield in France and landed in the grass between two bomb-cratered runways. A squad of Polish fighter planes offered to give them fuel to take off. They had started loading the fuel when they realized that the fighter fuel was a higher octane and would blow up the engines. They were then stuck there for several days until a unit of American tanks, which used the same fuel as the B-17, came along and gave them some of their fuel.

Norm would go on to fly another seventeen missions. His eighteenth mission would be his last. It was April 25, 1945, and also the 8th Air Force's very last mission of the war. They were flying to Pilzen, Czechoslovakia, that day and, after missing the target because of clouds, they circled around to make a second run. Allied propaganda had sent a message the previous day, notifying factory workers not to come to work, as the factories would be bombed. This had given the

Germans time to bring in more antiaircraft units, and the city was ringed with them. Norm's plane took a hit in the wing, leaving a hole the size of a bathtub. The pilot gave the order to bail out. Everyone bailed except the ball turret gunner,* who was having trouble getting out of his turret and getting his parachute attached properly. Norm wasn't about to leave the man behind and had started to help him when the plane went into a flat spin. The plane then exploded, blowing Norm out of the aircraft. He fell, unconscious, for 20,000 feet before coming to in time to pull his rip cord. He landed in a tree and had to cut his cords and fall another ten feet to reach the ground. Unable to collect his chute in order to bury and hide it, he moved away from it. While examining his injured arm, he looked up to see a group of German soldiers scrutinizing his chute. Fortunately they didn't search the area and instead continued on their way. Norm started walking back to where he figured the front lines were. He walked all night in stockinged feet—his boots had been blown off him in the explosion—until he came across a jeep full of GIs. They took him to a first aid station, and he eventually made it to a field hospital where he was properly treated.

The horrors of the war didn't end there for Norm, though. While recuperating, he was asked to be an eye witness for a group of medical personnel who were going to a prison camp. They went to Buchenwald concentration camp, and the experience and the sights were horrifying. One memory in particular that still haunts him was the moment he innocently opened the doors of one of the ovens to find half-burned bodies inside.

Norm spent some time in a hospital in England recuperating and finally returned home. One would think that after all he had been through, his service was finished. Instead, he was shipped to the West Coast, where he began training on a B-29 in preparation to head off to the Pacific Theater. Fortunately the war with Japan ended before that happened.

Almost sixty years after that fateful day over Pilzen, Norm received a phone call. The caller asked whether he had been over Pilzen that day, what the name of his plane was, and whether his plane had been shot down. Norm said yes, and the man said he had been looking for him. The man had been in the infantry and had watched as the plane got hit, the parachutes opened, and the plane exploded and crashed to the ground. He had gone to the crash site and picked up a piece of the plane, vowing to give it to the crew someday. They met a couple weeks later and while his memories of the crash had always been in the back of Norm's mind, holding that piece of the plane made those powerful memories come rushing forward. It was also a bonding experience for both men, and they have remained friends ever since.

*Charles Walker. He was the only crew member from Norm's plane killed that day. Norm thinks Walker may have been the last casualty of the war for the 8th Air Force as well.

Norm Markel Top row left

Ugly Memories

Mike Martinez grew up on a remote ranch and, like most people in pre-WWII America, had never traveled away from home. At age seventeen, he left school and enlisted in the Army. He was now traveling all over the United States for training and meeting people from different parts of the country.

After accelerated training, his unit, the 746th Field Artillery, loaded onto a ship for England. During the voyage they were hunted by German U-boats, and a number of times the men were told to report to the life rafts, as their commanders thought they were about to be torpedoed. After a short time in England, they crossed over to France in the fall of 1944. While in France they were once up to their knees in mud when along came a jeep carrying General Patton, who stopped and scolded the men about their appearance. He said it was not becoming to American soldiers and ordered them to clean themselves up.

The 746th moved north, and things got very bad, as the unit was caught up in the Battle of the Bulge. Everyone was ill prepared for this unexpected German offensive. The men didn't have enough ammunition or food, and they weren't adequately dressed for what was the coldest winter in fifty years. They were moving around in waist-deep snow, and their feet were freezing. Mike tears up as he remembers how they would take a blanket off a dead soldier and wrap their feet with it.

Death, destruction, and chaos were all around them. One time, while on the move, Mike's unit set up camp in the dark of night. At daybreak they found that the spot they had chosen was littered with dead German soldiers. Another time, one of the men was hit and was lying with his stomach split wide open. Mike ran to him, "put his guts back in him," covered him up, and stayed with him until he was evacuated. Mike narrowly escaped a similar fate once when he returned to a mess tent for a rare hot meal. An artillery shell landed five feet away from him, but fortunately it was a dud.

When the tide finally turned on the battlefield, things became relatively quiet for Mike, as the Germans were quickly being pushed back. He remembers being at the banks of the Danube River. It was a warm day, and he and some other soldiers had decided to go swimming, as they couldn't remember when they had last bathed. Across the river, the Germans were doing the same thing.

Things became ugly again when they came across a concentration camp, which Mike thinks was Dachau. They helped with the women's section. "I felt sorry for those women," Mike recalls. "Their heads were completely shaven, and they only had on thin cheese paper clothes. After all they had been through and then having to walk around naked in front of us strangers." The 746th continued on to Innsbruck, which is where they were when the war ended. Returning to Munich, they handled occupation duties until they accumulated enough points to return home.

The war did not end for Mike once he returned home. For many years he experienced flashbacks. He remembers how, when he first got married, his wife was startled when he flew out of bed after a bad dream and jumped out the window. Another time he was working out in a field when a crop duster flew over, and he dived into a ditch. He had one good postwar experience when the man whom he had helped save looked him up to thank him. After so many years of wondering whatever happened to that soldier, one ugly memory could now be erased.

Mike Martinez

A Dog Named Sue

Russ McConnell served as an officer with the 41st Field Artillery Battalion of the 3rd Infantry Division. His experiences started in French Morocco and then moved across Africa; there were amphibious landings in Sicily, Anzio, and southern France; there was service in Germany and then in Austria when the war ended. He is someone you could sit and listen to all day as he tells stories. But the story he wants to tell, the story that still tugs at his heart, is about a dog named Sue.

Russ began his association with Sue when he took over B Battery in France. He initially thought she was a stray they had picked up along the way, but she actually hailed from Tacoma, Washington. Her story began when a couple of men on leave from B Battery brought her back to the base at Ft. Ord, California, where pets were not allowed. Incredibly, the unit kept her hidden on the cross-country troop train to the East Coast and then on the ship to Africa! It is said that one of the men gave up space in his duffel bag to hide her.

Sue and B Battery were now in France. One night at battalion HQ, officers were sitting around talking about the various batteries, and they began running down B Battery. Russ spoke up and said that while the battery had its problems, it had potential. The next morning the colonel woke him up and addressed him as Baker 6, which was code for the leader of B Battery.

Now their new leader, Russ walked over to tell the battery the news, not knowing how he would be accepted. Sue, a terrier, was the first to greet him, and that was how he discovered that he was in charge of a unit of men and one dog. She quickly warmed up to him and her approval, coupled with Russ's explanation of how he got the command, broke the ice with the men.

Sue made her rounds daily, checking on the men. She seemed to sense that her duty was to maintain morale and give the men a brief reprieve from the war. Russ often thought as he watched Sue that for a brief moment she managed to transform a battle-hardened and weary soldier into a boy, sitting with his dog on the front porch back home. Sue also provided a soldier with toasty feet if his sleeping bag happened to be the one she decided to burrow into for the night.

Sue also sensed who the alpha dog of the battery was, as she always rode in Russ's jeep when they were on the move. On one occasion while in transit, the line of vehicles come to a halt, and Russ went to see what was up. The line began moving again, so Russ jumped back into his jeep. At their destination, he realized that Sue wasn't in the jeep and must have gotten out with him. This put him in a panic. "If I lose Sue, I will lose the battery," he thought. He sent some men back, and sure enough, Sue sat patiently waiting to be picked up at the spot where they had stopped.

Russ's assessment of the battery was borne out, as the battery became so well respected that it was given the honor of representing the American forces in a French Army awards ceremony. Unfortunately there wasn't enough room for the whole battery to participate in the parade, so many had to stay back, but a private walked up to Russ's jeep and, without asking permission from him, put Sue in the backseat, saying, "Sue, this is your seat." Sue rode proudly in the jeep past the viewing stand, where top brass and dignitaries sat.

Russ wonders how many awards Sue would have received, had she been human. "The division was in combat for 553 days and went through four amphibious landings and ten combat operations. Sue was there the entire way," he says, shaking his head. After the war, Sue returned home with one of the men, and Russ lost touch with her.

Russ is very proud of his service and feels privileged to have served with the 3rd Division—and with a small but mighty dog named Sue.

Russ McConnell

Sue

His Men

Money was very tight in Ben Mechling's home, as it was for many people caught in the grips of the Great Depression in the 1930s. His father had passed away a number of years earlier, which compounded the family's problems. As a result, Ben worked continuously whenever and wherever he could to bring in income for the family. When he enrolled in college, he sat out the fall semesters to work at a sugar beet factory. He also joined the National Guard to earn extra money.

Ben's unit was out on annual maneuvers with the Guard when Pearl Harbor was bombed, and it was soon nationalized, with the result that he was now in the Army. He started out in a tank destroyer battalion but didn't like it. He asked for, and was granted, a transfer to the Army Air Corps to become a pilot. He washed out of the pilot program, however, and returned to the regular Army. He decided to take some side courses on artillery and soon found himself commissioned as a lieutenant in charge of Battery C of the 232nd Field Artillery Battalion of the 42nd Infantry Division. The division shipped out for Europe and reached the Continent at Marseille, France. They would go on to fight throughout France and into Germany and on to Austria at the war's end.

The one thing you notice most about Ben when he talks about his experiences is just how much he talks about his men and how much he cared for them.

When they were first organizing and training in the States, Ben noticed that one of the men was clearly uneducated and had a terrible stuttering problem. He decided to take this man on as his driver so the other men would stop making fun of him. He also encouraged the soldier to continue his education. After the war, that man did continue his education and would go on to achieve an upper management position at a Fortune 500 company. He credits Ben with putting him on that track. They have remained friends ever since.

On the voyage across the Atlantic, Ben's comfortable officer's quarters sat topside, while his men traveled in cramped conditions down in the hull. Many of them were terribly seasick the entire time. Ben spent much of his time down in the hull with them, bringing them crackers and staying as long as he could stand it before the strong stench of vomit overtook him.

When they finally arrived on the battlefield, the welfare of his men continued to be paramount for Ben. On one occasion, while they were on the move, he stopped and refused to send any of his men farther until the area was checked for land mines. After considerable argument, another battalion leader behind Ben sent a jeep around him. Yards down the road the jeep hit a land mine, sending the passenger thirty feet into the air and killing him. The battalion leader then sent a second vehicle, and it too hit a land mine, which killed the driver.

"The one thing I am most proud about during my service is that I left with one hundred men, and I came back with those same hundred," Ben recalls. Very few leaders can say that. And anyone who might be tempted to accuse Ben of being overly cautious would be stopped by the Bronze Star, awarded for acts of bravery, that hangs in his medals shadow box.

Ben Mechling

Hold on! Hold on!

Images of the injured boys she treated still appear every time she hears the national anthem. Loud sounds make her flinch. She is still appreciative every time she climbs under the sheets in bed or takes a shower, with its seemingly endless supply of hot water. Her experiences as a combat nurse seventy years ago still conjure up strong feelings for Leila Morrison.

Leila knew at an early age that she wanted to be a nurse. This early ambition was spawned by what would turn out to be a lifelong enjoyment of helping people. Growing up the youngest of six and losing her mother at age three, her career choice didn't look promising, as her father was initially against it. He thought she was too small for the physical aspects of the job, but when she persisted in her ambitions, he eventually agreed to let her give nursing a try. She actually did so well in nursing school that she was asked to stay on as an instructor.

With the war now in full swing, Leila's world soon took a dramatic turn. Army recruiters came to the school one day and, feeling a strong sense of duty to serve, she enlisted in the Army Air Corps. Army training then took this girl from Blue Ridge, Georgia, across the country to Colorado, California, and finally to Texas, which became a pivotal point in her Army career as well as in her life, since this was where she trained to go overseas and also where she met a handsome Army officer.

Training involved such things as camping out in pup tents in the Texas scrub, an entirely new experience for Leila. Meeting that handsome officer happened at a dance. The 13th Armored Division based nearby hosted a dance and invited the nurses. Leila met Walt Morrison, and they hit it off, spending the entire evening together. After the dance that night, Walt, Leila, and Walt's jeep driver stopped at a café for a late-night bite to eat. The restaurant refused to serve Walt's driver, saying they didn't serve enlisted men. Walt then asked for three steak dinners to go, and they went outside and ate sitting on the curb. Later that night Walt told Leila that he loved her and that he would marry her someday. Leila laughed, telling him that he didn't even know her.

While Walt clearly saw their long-term future, the near term was an unknown. Both shipped out for overseas, uncertain where they were going. Leila took a train to New York and boarded a ship for Europe. She vividly remembers that she had started up the gang plank to the ship when a friend turned around and said, "We're not playing war anymore. We're heading to the real thing." Arriving in England as part of the 118th Evacuation Hospital, she undertook additional training before crossing the Channel to reach the Continent and the front lines. She remembers a humorous incident that occurred in England when a young child approached her group and asked her whether she was a "Yank." The question posed quite a dilemma for this Southern belle. She finally answered that yes, she was, and her friends laughed and never let her forget it.

Laughter became less and less common when they landed in France and began following the front lines. They were soon treating the wounded from the Battle of the Bulge during what proved to be one of the coldest winters in fifty years. The mobile hospital consisted of tents, and they constantly moved as the front did, twice ending up ahead of the front lines. Baths consisted of splashing cold water out of a helmet on themselves, and it would be a year before Leila actually took another hot shower. It was so cold at night that with only one blanket each, the nurses would double up in a cot so that they were both beneath two blankets.

On top of these harsh conditions, there was the stress of being in a war zone. Leila worked in the shock and pre-op tent, trying to keep the boys alive until they could get surgery or other treatments. Artillery shells often exploded overhead or nearby, making her jump. All these conditions left her mentally and physically spent, as well as frightened, but she refused to let her guard down and show it. "I had to keep my senses about me, as I didn't want the boys to see I was afraid. It would do them no good to see me frightened," she said. "I kept telling myself, 'Hold on! Hold on!'" The GIs were concerned about the safety of the nurses, and they often looked up at her and asked what she was doing there, worried that she was too close to the front lines. Leila says that she was prepared to die. Since she had lost her mother at age three and her father at twenty, and, given that she was single, she prayed to God to take her and spare the lives of the other nurses who had husbands and children.

Providing comfort to the wounded extended far beyond treating their physical wounds. Leila and the other nurses became surrogate mothers and sisters to the troops. They would sit and talk with them, helping them with their personal suffering as well. Leila remembers having many a soldier share photographs of his children with her—oftentimes when he had yet to meet those in the pictures. She helped with the emotional fallout after someone received a Dear John letter and sometimes simply held the hand of a boy far away from home and homesick. "The boys were so sweet, and they never complained," Leila notes in a tone filled with both sadness and affection.

If dealing with the horrors of war wasn't bad enough, it got worse when the hospital was called upon to help treat the prisoners from the Buchenwald concentration camp. On the first day of liberation, the doctors told the nurses to stay out because the conditions inside were so deplorable. Once they were allowed in, Leila could not comprehend what she was seeing. Thousands lay sick and dying, many completely covered by lice. A prisoner took her and others on a tour of the camp, showing them the crematorium. She calls the camp a factory of murder.

Amid all the ugliness she experienced during this time came some joy. Word came in that the 13th Armored Division had made camp right down the road. Soon Walt and other guys who had dated nurses in Texas showed up. With poor communications, and both having constantly been on the move, this was the first they had seen or heard from each other since leaving the States. Walt asked Leila to marry her, and she said she would not marry him until the war was over.

The Germans were finally defeated, and Leila found herself in France in one of the staging camps for the journey back home. Once again, by sheer luck, the 13th Armored was camped nearby, and once again she was reunited with Walt. He again asked her to marry him, and yet again she told him that she would not marry him until the war was over. Both were being sent back home for a thirty-day furlough and then possible deployment to the Pacific Theater.

Back in the States, they met up in Chicago. While they were there, Victory in Japan (VJ) Day occurred, and the war ended. Leila finally said yes. Two days later, when everything reopened after being shut down for a national celebration, they married. Walt and Leila spent sixty-five wonderful years together until his death.

Walt and Leila raised three children, and the family eventually added seven grandchildren and three great-grandchildren to its numbers. Walt owned a radio station, and Leila continued with her beloved nursing. The memories of her war experiences remain with her and are still strong. She has a recurring nightmare that the Germans chase and catch her; she sees the faces of the many boys she treated; and to this day she cannot take for granted the comforts of clean sheets and a hot shower. Still, she feels grateful for it all. "I am more than blessed. I am thankful that I was able to serve."

Leila Morrison

Mutual Love

"Making a mistake that might cost one of my men his life." That's Dale Peterson's answer when asked what the most frightening thing about the war was for him.

Dale graduated from Colorado A&M in 1942 and went off to the Army with three other buddies. They drove out to California in a car belonging to one of his buddies. The car's tires were bald, since, with wartime rationing and demand, they could not find tires anywhere. "We arrived at the base on inner tubes," Dale recalls. With his ROTC training, he left college with a commission. His mother, his biggest cheerleader throughout the war, said Hitler was going to realize he made a mistake going to war when he ran into the ROTC class of '42!

Dale joined up with the 936th Field Artillery of the 5th Army and after training shipped off for Africa. On the passage over, a boiler blew up, and everyone thought they had been torpedoed. Once in Africa, they traveled for four days across the desert. The one thing Dale remembers of this trip is the children he saw along the way. "I wish we could have gone back with some B-17s and bombed the area with Lifesaver candy for them," he says.

From Africa they sailed to Naples and first saw action at Cassino. The fighting was fierce. He remembers when they first began bombing a monastery. The men all climbed up on the roofs of houses to watch. As the planes began to fly over, everyone noticed that their bomb bay doors were opening too soon, and bombs were dropping prematurely. They all scrambled to shelters before the errant bombs hit.

The 936th left Cassino for Rome, and along the way Dale was given command of A Battery, a unit with a very poor performance record. The men openly celebrated in front of their old commander when the news was announced. Dale quickly understood what the problem was. His first statement to them was that he would do his job and leave them alone to do theirs. The battery's performance quickly turned around.

Dale saw his job as taking care of the men. His worst day in the war, which still brings a sob from him, was when a man couldn't take it anymore and tried to commit suicide. Dale rushed to his side to offer aid and comfort. He was severely reprimanded by his higher-ups for leaving his command post to comfort that man.

But leaving his post to go to his men was common practice for him, though his men thought he was crazy for doing it. Oftentimes during artillery barrages, Dale ran from dugout to dugout to make sure his men were all right. Once during a barrage, there was an explosion, and clothes flew everywhere. Dale's heart dropped, for he thought that one of his men's dugouts had taken a direct hit. He eventually found out that a shell had hit a duffel bag full of laundry.

Dale returned home after the war, married, raised a family, and went on to be a successful farmer. His farm was once highlighted in a PBS documentary. Dale never did realize his worst fear of the war: though a few were wounded, he didn't lose any men. One of his sergeants visited Dale on his farm after the war. Dale commented on how much he loved and respected those men, and the sergeant said, "Dale, the feeling was mutual. Those men loved you and would have followed you into hell."

Dale Peterson

In a Frozen Hole

Walter Sapp sat in his foxhole thinking about the war. He did a lot of thinking there. Oftentimes the thinking revolved around whether he would make it through the night to see the morning sunrise. One night he was thinking about the war in general. "I remember thinking, my dad was over here fighting in World War I, and now I am here. What the hell is wrong with these people?" he recalls.

He had these thoughts during the Battle of the Bulge. He and his division, the 78th Infantry, were surrounded on three sides by Germans. It was one of the coldest winters in Europe's history, and he didn't have the proper winter clothing and had very little food. He doesn't remember finally getting out of that foxhole, as he had to be lifted out of it because his feet were frozen solid. The next thing he remembers is waking up in a hospital in Luxembourg, uncertain whether it was Allied or German. They were able to thaw out his feet and save them, and after recovering, he returned to his unit.

The Battle of the Bulge, the largest and bloodiest battle fought in World War II, was now over, and the Germans were in retreat. The 78th began quickly moving eastward and reached the Rhine River at the town of Remagen. The bridge there was wired with explosives by the Germans to prevent the Americans from crossing it, as it was the last standing bridge over the Rhine. The Germans set off the charges, but the bridge didn't come down. (Those put in charge of destroying the bridge were immediately rounded up, tried, and executed by the Nazis.) Taking the bridge was a huge development in the war, since it allowed American forces to cross a major natural obstacle and move into Germany proper. With his battle experience and knowledge, Walter was chosen to carry all the company commander's papers and maps, and he would be one of the first to cross the bridge! It was touch and go for a time until enough men and equipment finally crossed the river to establish a strong bridgehead.

In Walter's estimate, being able to rush equipment, material, and men across the bridge shaved months off the war. German morale seemed to drop, even though they were now fighting on their own soil—and still fighting hard. The war would go on for another two months, and Walter still saw plenty of action. While trying to take a castle on a hill, his unit was taking both enemy fire and friendly artillery fire. The unit leader was killed and the radioman badly injured. Walter grabbed the radio, and the radioman was telling him how to use it when he also died. Walter figured out how to use the radio and was able to redirect the artillery fire.

Casualties were high because at this point in the war more and more inexperienced replacement soldiers and officers were being sent to the front, and they simply didn't have the keen sense of being in battle that Walter and other battle-hardened soldiers had developed. He remembers a unit of African-American soldiers with whom he spent the night in a castle. The next morning, as they left, Walter recalls thinking that they had no idea what they were in for and that they didn't have enough training. He later heard that the whole unit was wiped out.

Along the way, the 78th liberated a work camp. Walter was shocked by the barbaric conditions of the camps and the "walking skeletons" inhabiting it. He still can't understand how such an advanced people, particularly in the sciences, could do to their fellow man the things he saw.

The Germans finally surrendered in May, and soon after, the 78th was sent to Berlin to represent the United States. While there, Walter had access to a jeep, and he visited the damaged Reich Chancellery. The Russians guarding it allowed him to enter. He toured the inside and then stepped out onto the balcony where Hitler had once stood. There he was, he thought, a nineteen-year-old from rural Ohio, standing in the same place that one of the world's most powerful men once stood. Later, during his stint in Berlin as part of the occupation forces, he watched the Russians recreate and film the taking of the Chancellery.

As Walter sits here thinking about the war, he says that one thing that left a very strong impression on him was the incredible heroism and bravery he saw all along the way. An example of this occurred during the battle when he took over the radio. Walter saw a man whose arm had nearly been blown off leading his men up the hill, the remnants of his arm dangling from the socket. Walter also thinks about the historical aspect of what he was part of and what he witnessed. He was in the Bulge; he was one of the first to cross the Rhine; and he stood on Hitler's balcony—earning a Bronze Star in the process. On this day, as he reflects on the war, the best thing, he says, is that he is doing so on a comfortable couch and not in a frozen foxhole.

Walter Sapp

Paid Dearly

Wayne Seaman had a very busy week in April of 1943. "I graduated from Colorado A&M, got married, and went off to the Army all in one week," Wayne recalls with a chuckle.

Because he was at a land grant university, Wayne was involved with ROTC on campus. This ROTC experience, coupled with a college degree, made him a candidate for Officer Candidate School, and he shipped off to Fort Sill, Oklahoma. After getting his commission as a lieutenant, he was assigned to the 94th Armored Field Artillery Battalion of the 4th Armored Division. In late December he shipped overseas, spending both Christmas and New Year's at sea on the rough, cold Atlantic.

He landed in England and for the next six months had additional training and maneuvers. This also allowed him to take leaves in London, where he saw firsthand the damage caused by the German Blitz bombing. On one occasion he was actually caught in a bomb raid while visiting the city. Curiosity brought him outside to watch the raid, until shrapnel from the antiaircraft guns started showering down on him, and he thought it best to go back into the bomb shelter. D-Day occurred in June of 1944, and the 4th Armored followed two weeks later.

They landed at Normandy with the beaches still full of broken-up equipment. The beachhead was only about eight miles inland at this time. Hedgerows, which are large mounds of rocks, dirt, thick brush, and trees, surrounded all the fields in the area, making it a difficult place for tank warfare. Wayne didn't think he would make it out of there. In order to break out, everyone backed up about a half mile from the front lines, and a massive wave of bombers came over and bombed the Germans. The bombing was so intense that Wayne and his men, lying under their tanks watching the bombing, were bouncing off the ground from the vibrations. Finally they were liberated, and the war started moving across France.

With the position of forward observer, Wayne had a front row seat from which to observe much of the fighting. He often sat in his tank and watched the dogfights going on above him. Because he was so close to the front lines, he had to put fluorescent pink panels on the back of his tank so that he wouldn't come under friendly fire. Being both a tanker and that close to the front lines, the odds eventually caught up with Wayne.

He was injured twice. The first injury was minor enough that he was patched up in the field. The second one took him out of the war. His tank took a direct hit, which ripped through the machine. Burned and with a badly broken leg, he was barely able to pull himself out of the tank. One other crew member was also able to get out, but three others died. Wayne received two Purple Hearts for his injuries. He was also awarded the Silver Star, the third-highest medal a serviceman can be awarded.

Wayne would pay dearly for his service. He would go on to spend the next year and a half in the hospital recovering, nearly losing his leg. Once he returned home, he wanted to get into the forest service. He took the forestry exam and scored the second highest in the nation, but because of his war injuries, he failed the physical exam. He then went back to school and earned a master's in game management and would go on to have a long career as a fish biologist.

Wayne Seaman

Small-Town Girl

As Leonie went about her work in the map room, she felt that she was just a small-town girl doing an ordinary job. But there was nothing ordinary about her situation. She was in wartime London working for the Office of Strategic Services (OSS), the forerunner of today's CIA.

Just a short time earlier, she would never, in her wildest dreams, have thought she would be here. She grew up in the small, central Louisiana town of Mansura. She and her family struggled through the Depression, and then she went off to college, afterward landing a job teaching high school math and science. It was during this time that two events changed her life.

The first was meeting Leo Shannon. They met at a dance organized for the soldiers at a nearby base. Her mother helped chaperone the dance. Her mother had met Leo earlier and played matchmaker, setting up him and Leonie. But Poor Leo started out with two strikes against him. First, Leonie didn't care for her own name, and Leo's was similar to hers. Second, he couldn't dance and stepped all over her feet on the dance floor. He eventually must have hit one out of the park, however, as Leonie did indeed fall in love with the handsome soldier.

The second event was the arrival of an Army recruiter at the high school to talk to the teachers. Leonie was surprised that the principal allowed it, but she now thinks he probably had no choice. The Army was looking for women to fill the ranks of the newly formed Women's Army Corps. Leonie's sense of adventure kicked in, and she enlisted and shipped off to Georgia for training. This adventure truly ramped up when, because she was fluent in French, she was one of forty women chosen to be sent to London as a special attachment to the OSS.

She soon found herself crossing the Atlantic aboard the luxury liner, the *Queen Elizabeth*, which had been converted into a troop ship. One night during the crossing, everyone was tossed back and forth in their bunks all night long. When they compared notes the next morning, they learned that the ship was zigzagging ahead of a German U-boat that was chasing them. They landed in Glasgow, and from there Leonie took a train down to London. Here she found that she would be living in an elegant mansion and working in a British intelligence building on Baker Street, the street made famous by the Sherlock Holmes novels.

London was a very different environment from what Leonie was accustomed to, but being at war greatly augmented the strangeness of her surroundings. It was pitch-black at night, as there were blackouts because of the German bombings. The first time Leonie was in a bombing raid, she was terribly frightened. She describes how she quickly became a Londoner, though, growing accustomed to the bombings. She remembers clearly one day walking down a street when a German V2 rocket flew across the sky. She stopped to stare up at it, becoming mesmerized by it. When she looked back down, she realized that she was the only person on the street. Many years later, she was able to see a V2 up close in a museum.

Leonie's job in the map room involved her getting decoded messages from France reporting the status of agent and supply drops into Nazi-occupied France the previous day. Leonie would then mark the information on the large map of France. A sad part of the job was marking unsuccessful operations, as the agents were often shot in the air or once they landed. Many times agents would come into the map room to study the map before their missions. Leoni remembers one young man in particular. "I don't think we even said a word to each other, but I was very impressed by him," Leoni remembers. She was deeply saddened when she learned the next day that he had been killed. It is an incident that still brings tears to her eyes nearly seventy years later.

Another event that still brings tears to her eyes, when she thinks of all the men who were lost, is D-Day. It was such a secret operation that even she and her coworkers didn't know when it was to happen, although they sensed that an important operation was imminent because there was an increase in the number of high-ranking officials visiting the map room. She knew the operation must be under way when she heard a loud, continuous drone and went outside to see the skies almost black with planes flying eastward.

A memory that brings a smile to Leonie's face is of the time when a high-ranking official visited the map room. General William ("Wild Bill") Donovan, head of the OSS, visited and pinned medals on the women. Everyone was at attention when he announced that he wished he was French so he could kiss every woman on each cheek. This made all the women swoon. "Gen. Donovan was known as a rascal," Leonie says, smiling.

During Leonie's time in London, her mother worried. Because Leonie couldn't tell anyone what she was doing, her mother was certain she had—or would—become an agent. And seeing the bombings of London on the newsreels at home didn't help things. Leonie wrote home often to assure her mother that she was okay. But unlike the split-second communications we have today via the Internet, communications via the mail could be weeks apart.

Leonie had her own worries as well, and the slow communications did not help matters. During this time Leo had been sent to Africa and from there up through Italy. It was a long-distance relationship in the extreme: a courtship conducted across three continents. From Africa Leo had his father in the States send Leonie an engagement ring in London.

Once the D-Day landing was successful, and the Allies freed France, Leonie was no longer needed in London, and she was transferred back to the States. She would serve with the Air Corps, where, until she was discharged, she helped airman prepare for, and apply to, college.

Leo eventually made it back home safely, and the two married. She would go on to teach school for twelve years, and Leo went into the grocery business. They were married for fifty-five years until Leo passed away, and they had four children—sadly, losing a son at age two—and three grandchildren.

Leonie looks back today with fondness and pride in her service. She also realizes now that yes, she was a small-town girl, but it was no ordinary job she did; it was an important position, and she did her part in the effort to win the war.

Leonie Shannon

Never Forgetting

"Sir, there's a hole big enough that I could stick my fist in it!" That was the response Wayne Tennant got from one of his men when he asked the soldier to check a wound Wayne had received in his back when he was hit with shrapnel during an artillery attack. The piece of metal that tore into his back and embedded itself in his chest cavity landed up in a picture frame on a wall in his office.

That picture frame also contained other mementos of Wayne's service during World War II: the Bronze Star, the Purple Heart, other medals and patches, and his dog tags. It was service that started in the prewar draft prior to Pearl Harbor and didn't end until five years later.

Wayne grew up in rural Nebraska and received his draft notice in February of 1941. It was supposed to be a one-year term. "One and done" was what it was called, but when Pearl Harbor was attacked, it was extended to "open-ended." With the rush to build up an army, coupled with Wayne's time already served, he was given the opportunity to go to officer's training school. He was then given command of Co. C, 705th Tank Destroyer Battalion. After training, Wayne and the battalion shipped off to Europe.

After arriving in England, they began training and planning for action on the Continent, and Wayne always remembered when D-Day began. "Looking up into the sky, it was nothing but solid airplanes of all kinds flying east," he recalled. His battalion followed shortly after, landing in France and beginning a journey that would take them into Belgium, the Netherlands, Germany, and finally Austria, at the war's end. When the Battle of the Bulge began, the 705th raced to Bastogne to help out the 101st Airborne. It was here that Wayne was wounded, and since they were completely surrounded by the Germans, it took seven days to get him evacuated to England for proper treatment, which meant surgery.

Wayne spent two months in the hospital recovering from his wounds. During this time, the hospital received a letter from General Eisenhower's headquarters. Because of the respect and admiration they had for Wayne, the men of his battalion had sent a letter directly to Eisenhower, requesting that Wayne be returned to their unit if he was able to return to duty. It was an unheard-of request, but it was granted, and Wayne did recover enough to rejoin his battalion.

But Wayne returned to a battalion he barely recognized. One third of the 600-man battalion had either been injured or killed. Three of his fellow company commanders had lost limbs and were gone. The battalion continued on through Germany, saw the horrors of the concentration camps when it liberated the Mauthausen camp, and finished up in Austria with mop-up and occupation duties when the war in Europe finally came to an end.

But the memories of the war never ended for Wayne. He was haunted by them for a long time after he returned home, although it became somewhat better over time. He described it all as a bad nightmare. Although he tried to forget these bad memories, the memory of his battalion was one he wanted to keep alive for others to know about. He was the president of the 705th Association until he died. He kept in touch with surviving members and/or their families, put out a newsletter, and was the keeper of the battalion's history. Like he did during the war, he was doing his part to take care of his battalion and keep it together.

Wayne Tennant

Screaming Mimis

Robert Todd left to serve in the Army seventeen days after his first son was born. Fortunately he had a furlough and was home when his second child, a daughter, was born, but he shipped out for overseas five days later. It would then be a year and a half before he would see his family again.

Bob served with the 21st Armored Infantry Battalion of the 11th Armored Division. He joined up with his unit after that last furlough, and they boarded a ship for Europe. After a stay in England, where they received additional training, they crossed the Channel to France. They entered the war just as the Battle of the Bulge started.

Bob drove a wrecker in the unit that kept the vehicles operating and moving. He was often pulling out a stuck half-track truck or working on a truck in the thick of battle. He once got an overturned half-track upright and moved, only to look back and see a shell land and explode right where he had just been. The worst was always when the "Screaming Mimi" attacks came. The screaming Mimi was an artillery shell that made a screaming sound as it came in. "They made a terrifying sound," Bob recalls.

The 11th fought across Germany and turned south to Austria, where they were stopped to await the approaching Russians. One time Bob had to go into the Russian sector to retrieve a vehicle. "It was pretty hairy there for a while. I was completely surrounded by Russians as they climbed all over my truck. They had never seen a wrecker before."

Prior to meeting the Russians and the war's end, the 11th also helped liberate Mauthausen concentration camp. What Bob saw was horrifying. "Those still barely alive were walking skeletons. The dead were stacked up like cords of wood," Bob says, shaking his head.

Naturally his family was always on his mind. He and his wife, Ione, wrote each other often, and in one of her letters she included a picture of her and the two children. He looked at that picture every day. He remembers guys from the unit looking at the picture. "They would always say, 'Bob, you're so lucky,'" Bob recalls, his eyes welling up with tears. Back home, Ione worried about Bob, and because his letters were censored, she listened to the radio reports of the war and read the newspapers to try to glean any information she could.

The war finally ended, and Bob stayed through the summer with the occupation forces until he had enough points to come home. During this time, he had the opportunity to visit Hitler's hideaway in the Alps. He remembers wondering how such a beautiful place could house such an evil person.

Bob returned home to Kansas and his young family. While he was happy and relieved to be home, it was an adjustment. Ione remembers a man who was always jolly before the war. Her husband came home very serious and couldn't sleep. She recalls one incident when he was out milking a cow. He had always whistled beautifully, and she was trying to learn to whistle too. She came up behind him whistling, and he jumped up, kicking over the milk bucket, yelling, "Ione, don't ever do that again!" she recalls. He finally explained that her whistling sounded like a Screaming Mimi.

Bob farmed for seven years and then went on to a twenty-seven-year career with the Postal Service. He and Ione have been married for seventy years, and that young family he left behind to go off to war has now grown to four children, seven grandchildren, and eleven great-grandchildren.

Robert Todd

The picture he looked at every day.

Front Row Seat

Ted Wahler had a front row seat during the war from the time he entered Marseille, shortly after the invasion of southern France, and continuing through the Battle of the Bulge and his entry into Germany and finally Austria, when the war ended.

Ted served with the 141st Ordnance Medium Maintenance Company, which had an instrument repair unit that fixed range finders, binoculars, scopes, etc. He was on a three-man team that went to the front lines to evaluate the condition of equipment that might need repair and was embedded with the front-line infantry.

That front row seat came with its share of danger and close calls, and his team carried a grenade under the seat of their specialized repair truck with orders to blow it up if they were ever captured. On one occasion, while sleeping in a bombed-out house with some of the front-line soldiers, he got up in the middle of the night to relieve himself. Half-asleep, he was about to walk out the front door when a hand slipped over his mouth and pulled him back in, just as a German patrol walked by. A number of times infantrymen pulled him down and lay over him before incoming shells hit. "Those doughboys saved my life numerous times," Ted recalls gratefully. Another time he sat on the top of a German pillbox on the Maginot Line and watched as US troops advanced across a field toward a village. He later learned that there were still Germans inside the pillbox.

While he was often on the front lines, Ted admits that he feels grateful that he never had to shoot anyone. Well, with the exception of one incident. During the Battle of the Bulge, there was chaos everywhere. Everyone was on edge, as the Germans had infiltrated the American lines and were using American uniforms and vehicles, changing road signs around, and generally creating havoc. One night Ted was on guard duty when he heard rustling in the dark. He gave the password but got no response. After numerous attempts to get the intruder to come out, he shot his Thompson submachine gun in the general direction of the rustling and heard a moan. Later, he found out that he had shot a cow. What would follow was a nice steak dinner for his unit and a lot of ribbing for Ted.

Ted never worried about the dangerous situations he was in because he had vowed when he left the States that he would make it back alive, and he maintained that conviction throughout his service. When he returned to America from Europe, he had lost that feeling. The war was still raging with Japan, and his company had orders to ship off to the Pacific. "I was so certain I would not come back alive. In fact, I returned home to Buffalo on a furlough specifically to say my good-byes," he says. Fortunately, while he was home on that furlough, Japan surrendered.

After his service, Ted took a couple months off to decompress at his family's vacation lake cottage. He would eventually accept a job that took him overseas to Saudi Arabia. While there he met a woman named Pearl, who was also working on an overseas assignment and who would become his wife. They married in Switzerland and honeymooned in a post-war Europe. Returning to the States, Ted used his mechanical skills in a career in product development with Lego Toys. In the last year of his life, Ted was on his way to the send-off ceremony with Honor Flight to take his seat on a trip to honor his WWII experience when he got very ill. Unfortunately he never recovered to take that wonderful trip.

Ted Wahler

Spoiled Milk

Chuck Winston turned eighteen while out working in Kansas. He returned home to Colorado because he wanted to be inducted into the service in Colorado. The aftermath of his father's own service was what had brought his family to Colorado when Chuck was young.

Chuck's father had served in World War I and was gassed. That, coupled with the influenza he contracted during the epidemic of 1918, caused him to develop tuberculosis. The doctor suggested he move to Colorado and even then only gave him a year to live. The family moved to Colorado, and the climate must have agreed with him, as he lived to be sixty-nine.

Chuck was inducted into the Army and, after Stateside training, he caught a troop ship to Europe, landing in Le Havre, France. He arrived in February of 1945 at the tail end of the Battle of the Bulge when the Allies had the Germans on the run. Chuck joined the front lines as a replacement in the 261st Infantry Regiment in the 65th Infantry Division under Patton's 3rd Army. The 65th raced across Germany and down to Austria, stopping at the Enns River. It was there that they met up with the Russians, just as the war in Europe ended. "I was very lucky that I didn't see as much action as a lot of soldiers did," Chuck says. He saw and experienced enough, though—experiences he does not want to talk about—and for many years afterward he continued to experience nightmares.

One of the more pleasant experiences he still laughs about was once checking out the cellar of an Austrian farmhouse, where the troops found a family cowering in fear. When they realized it was the Americans, they became very happy and started hugging them. They also filled the soldiers' canteens with fresh cow's milk. The troops began the move onward again, with their packs tied onto the sides of their trucks. Chuck's truck clipped a corner of a building and ripped all the packs off. Much later on, after Germany had surrendered, and the war was over, Chuck went into Supply to turn in some equipment.

The supply officer said, "Winston? Winston? I think I have something of yours." He came back with Chuck's canteen. It still contained the milk, by now long spoiled!

With the war now over, Chuck began occupation duties. He was able to travel during his furloughs and once had the opportunity to see Hitler's Eagle's Nest. He soon deployed back to the States with plans to continue on to the Pacific Theater where the war was still raging. Fortunately, the day his troop ship landed back in Norfolk, Virginia, VJ Day was announced.

After his service, Chuck returned home and married Dorothy. They had planned on traveling when they retired, and she had been putting money away for a trip to Europe. Sadly, however, Chuck lost Dorothy in 1992. He and his son would take the trip that she had planned, retracing Chuck's steps in the service. Chuck's son represents the third generation of Winstons to serve our country, having served in the Vietnam War.

Chuck Winston

Life as a Waist Gunner

Statistically the most dangerous place to be in World War II was in a bomber over Europe. Henry Yekel managed to beat the odds to come home alive and physically unscathed. He flew thirty official missions as a waist gunner in a B-17 with the 340th Bomb Squad, 97th Bomber Group of the 15th Air Force.

Henry entered the Army shortly after he graduated from high school. Scoring very high in testing, he was sent to cadet school to become a pilot. Well into the training, he was the victim of what he calls a bad April Fool's joke when the Air Corps announced that they had enough pilots, and the program was being discontinued. Given the opportunity to go on to anything he wanted to do, he asked what would get him into the action the most quickly, and the answer to this question landed him in gunnery school.

He found himself crisscrossing the country to various bases for training. While stationed in Lincoln, Nebraska, he asked a cute girl in a crowded bowling alley whether he could bowl with her. Soon after, he formed up with a crew and headed off for Europe with the 97th. They set up a base in Foggia, Italy, and began flying missions.

Flying in a bomber is no picnic. It is extremely loud, the interior isn't pressurized, and with the bomb bay doors and open windows for machine guns, it can get as cold as sixty degrees below zero. These conditions require the crew to wear layers of clothes, electrically heated suits, oxygen masks, and flak jackets—about one hundred pounds' worth of equipment. The actual missions over enemy territory aside, flying in a bomber is simply dangerous. Bad weather, mechanical breakdowns, and flying in very close formations cause many accidents.

On Henry's thirty missions, a mix of milk runs (easy missions) and dangerous runs, he had many close calls. He remembers one of his first missions, where the plane ran into a heavy flak attack. When they landed, the crew started counting the holes in the plane and gave up at 200. Returning home from another mission, the crew reported that they were having trouble with the oxygen system. The ground crew checked it out, and they couldn't find anything wrong. When they were assigned the same plane on the next mission, the pilot refused to fly it, citing the danger. They were then told to switch with another crew. Shortly after the formation got into the air, the tail gunner reported that the plane they were initially supposed to take had burst into flames and was in a nosedive. On another mission Henry was feeding strips of foil, used to fool German radar, down a tube. The other gunner was handing him the strips, which were about a foot long. He looked at the strips he was holding, which were only four inches long. He then looked up at the other gunner, who had the other ends in his hand. A piece of flak had ripped through the plane and cut the strips in half.

As awful as they were, he has one fond memory of the flak attacks by the Germans. Normally the flak bursts (clouds filled with chunks of metal) were either black or white. Once, on a Christmas Day mission, the flak shells burst into clouds of red and green.

Returning home after the war's end, Henry started college and worked for thirteen years in retail and three years with the postal service, capping it all off with a twenty-three-year career at the National Bureau of Standards. Oh, and that cute girl in the bowling alley? Henry returned to Lincoln and married her. He and Mary were married for sixty-six years until his death.

Henry Yekel

Closing Thoughts

It is said that the best education is found sitting at the feet of an elder. I have learned so much sitting with these people. Not just about history, but about life in general. We have so much to learn from this generation—from their experiences, their wisdom, their knowledge, their philosophies, and their ethics.

Many of the people I interviewed for this book became instant friends whom I care about and with whom I keep in touch. The pleasure I have found in meeting and knowing them is now coupled with sadness as they begin passing. And as they pass, I despair that we will never see another generation like theirs. I feel truly blessed that I have crossed paths with them.

We must never forget these people and what they did.

About the Book

The men and women interviewed in this book endured back-to-back crises early on in their lives. The first was the Great Depression. The second was World War II. They were just kids—seventeen, eighteen, nineteen years old—when they went off to war, where many were put into roles where they had tremendous responsibility. Often they were thrown into hellish situations. Far too early and far too quickly, they were robbed of their youth and innocence. Over sixteen million of them served and, bolstered by a united home front, they won the war on two massive fronts, helping to save the world. They returned home and, without skipping a beat, moved on with their lives. Not wanting their children to endure what they did in their youth, they put their noses to the grindstone and built this country's economy into the largest the world has ever seen. Truly the greatest generation. Now in their eighties and nineties, these veterans of WWII tell their stories, many for the first time, providing a fresh, human perspective on the war.

About the Author

Brad began preserving the stories of veterans because of his love of history, his interest in hearing people tell their stories, and his awe and deep respect for what our World War II veterans did and continue to do. What started out for him as a simple project, with the aim of collecting these stories, has grown into an all-consuming quest to honor veterans in whatever way he can. In addition to working on his veteran's history project, he volunteers for Honor Flight and is on a committee that helped build a veterans plaza to honor veterans. Brad lives in Windsor, Colorado.

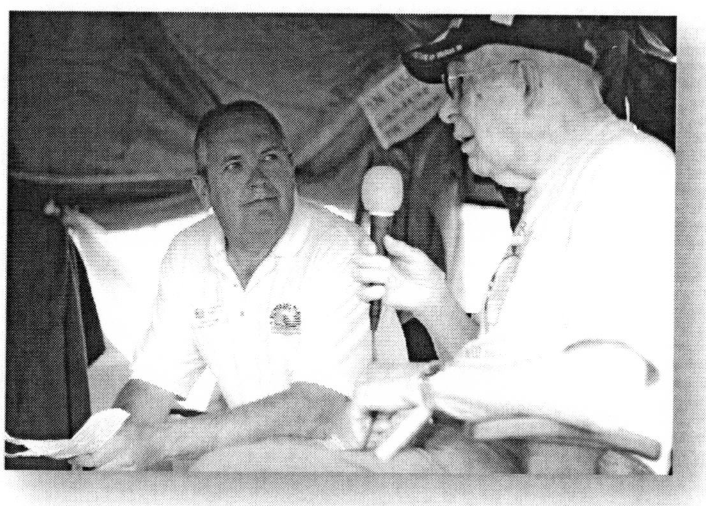

Brad Hoopes (photo courteous of Lee Cooper)

If you would like to learn more about Brad's veterans history project, or would like to get a DVD copy of the full interview of any of the veterans in this book, please visit his website:

www.rememberandhonor.com

CPSIA information can be obtained
at www.ICGtesting.com
Printed in the USA
FFOW02n1916170517
35749FF

9 781634 908252